Playing It By Ear

Adam's upcycled builds on a budget

HERE
NOW
BOOKS

First published in Great Britain in 2024
by Here Now Books
https://herenowbooks.co.uk

ISBN 978-1-0686149-0-3

Designed and typeset by Helius

Photographs of the Big Green Bus and Evergreen Cabin used with kind
permission of Samantha Pells Photography.

Photographs and words of George Clarke used with his kind permission.

Photograph of the author by Annie Armitage at anniearmitage.com

Playing It By Ear
Adam's upcycled builds on a budget

Mima Biddulph

With a foreword by George Clarke

Acknowledgements

We both have people to thank. Adam, want to go first?

OK. Thank you to...
   Egg (Enfys) for her never-wavering support in the face of a very difficult past few years – she gave me the strength to push on.
   Devon, who has grown into a brilliant human I'm incredibly proud of.
   My family, especially my mum, Evelyn, for her support and for bailing me out without question.
   My friends, especially Mima whose schoolteacher training kept me in line and on topic while putting this book together, and George for his kind words of support and friendship.
   And lastly to Salbo for a lifetime of ongoing loyalty. I love that stinky mutt. x
Over to you, Mima.

Thank you to...
   Simon Waller for many things but especially for encouraging me to stick it to the Man.
   My mum, Marie Griffiths, for everything. I'd like her to get on with her own writing now because I want to read it. Shout out to my children: Felix for the website and Clementine for the graphics advice, and to my whole family for their encouragement and practical assistance.
   My friends, especially Oliver James for his support and for taking me seriously, and Adam, for trusting me and for introducing me to Fortuna.
   Writers CBC Massive for being right behind me...look, they can't stop us!
   Julie and Rich at Helius for their experienced midwifery skills (copy-editing, typesetting, cover art, proofreading and morale) in the world of books and for their patience with a primigravida.
   Bookvault printers for holding the gate open.
   Agatha Christie dedicated *The Secret Adversary* 'To all those who lead monotonous lives, in the hope that they may experience at second hand the delights and dangers of adventure.' I'll dedicate this book to all those who foolhardily experience those delights and dangers at first hand, especially those who come late to the party or need a little push.

Contents

George Clarke and Adam Collier-Woods outside the newly built Big Green Bus

Foreword

In 2012, we made and broadcast the first ever season of *George Clarke's Amazing Spaces*. Any first season is always an enormous risk. Of course, you have the big idea of what you want to make (ours was 'Let's make a series about people making small spaces') but the truth is you don't really know what the final programme is going to look and feel like – and you certainly have no idea whether people are going to watch it. We didn't even have a title for the series until we were 90% of the way through our filming schedule.

The same can be said for many of the projects that feature in the series. Our contributors have the big idea of what they want to do, but rarely know how they are going to do it or exactly what the final build is actually going to look like.

Luckily, series 1 was a resounding success and in 2013 we began casting for contributors and their amazing builds for series 2. We needed to select eight projects from hundreds of applications. One particular story jumped out at me from the pages of our casting document: a bloke called Adam wanted to convert a double-decker bus into a mini 'glamping' home for surfing breaks. I watched his casting tape and knew within seconds that we had to follow his story.

Adam has a wonderful creative mind. A creative mind is not afraid to investigate new ideas; it is open to all possibilities and operates without conventional boundaries. It can also be a bag of contradictions: on the one hand driven, focused and realistic; on the other naive, an imaginative dreamer.

Luckily, Adam isn't just a creative thinker – he is also a creative builder. He can be incredibly practical and can turn his hands to making beautiful things. This combination of limitless exploratory ideas and the skills to realise the elements of a build in material form is a thing of joy and wonder.

Of course, any creative journey Adam goes on is a rollercoaster ride of indecisions, decisions, knowns and unknowns. You're never sure what you are going to get until the project is fully complete. That is the beauty of his way of working. He is an architectural rebel, pushing the boundaries of designing and building to produce structures that are unique and playful.

His Big Green Bus was wonderful: a masterclass in creativity. It brought joy to so many people as well as much needed income for Adam. Unfortunately, the life of the bus came to a sad end when it caught fire, but Adam never gave up.

I have to say it was an honour and a privilege to film him again ten years later, for the 12th series of *Amazing Spaces*. This time he built his Evergreen Cabin – a majestic cabin in the woods made from transformed shipping containers, repurposed objects and recycled materials.

Adam is a kind and sensitive soul, but he is also an *Amazing Spaces* warrior who has battled through many difficult challenges, including his illness, to achieve what others would struggle to pull off.

I admire Adam so much and I'm proud to call him a good friend. This is his story and I'm glad to have been a small part of it.

George Clarke

George Clarke and Adam Collier-Woods outside the newly built Evergreen Cabin

Introduction

We're taught from a young age to prepare, to be cautious and think ahead. We're supposed to walk before running, look before leaping, be safe not sorry. My friend Adam's parents tried to teach him all that but it never worked, and he doesn't regret it because the more he sees of life the more he thinks many people are too careful, their lives limited by fear of failure. Dread of ridicule, unease about the unknown and horror of making mistakes are inhibiting. As a result, we might not try new things, take enough risks or put unconventional ideas into practice. It seems a shame: if his namesake Adam Ant has taught us anything it's that ridicule is nothing to be scared of.

Don't get me wrong: there are probably wiser, better ways to do most of the things Adam's done – I won't pretend nothing's ever gone wrong, but he's stubbornly kept going through countless attempts to thwart his efforts, foil his plans and dampen his enthusiasm. These have come from all quarters: the elements, thieves, fools, liars, illness, bad luck and, he'll freely admit, himself, lobbing spanners in the works with mischievous glee. Even thoroughly nice people with the best of intentions have been known to rain on his parade while trying to protect him from himself.

The sensible, safe thing is to give in or not to try in the first place, but where's the fun in that? There have been problems, but Adam's upcycling adventures have been well worth it and he's learned new skills, seen new places and met great people along the way. Thousands of lovely guests have enjoyed staying on his bus and in the cabin, and his homes and holidays in boats and vans have given him some of his favourite memories.

Life's too short for him to become an expert at everything before he even tries it – he prefers to get started, play it by ear and adapt as he goes along, fixing it in the mix. I've known the project king, as I sometimes call him, most of my life and have always loved his approach in theory, but find myself more hesitant in reality. Digging into his story to write this book, however, has inspired me to be braver, which is why you're getting to read it.

This is the story of how Adam ended up on the telly many times and created an income, despite living with Ménière's disease, by turning vehicles and storage containers into homes. So, if you sometimes feel like throwing caution to the wind, but you want evidence that fortune favours the brave, read on...

Simon, behind best man Adam, behind Mima, at Simon and Mima's wedding, 1999

- 1 -
Informal Apprenticeship
Enterprises and antics before the bus

The Big Green Bus, a holiday home in an old double-decker, became a phenomenon beyond anything Adam had ever expected. Having the idea seemed to prompt a snowballing momentum that just kept growing, gaining interest, popularity and bookings. The journey was hard work and he made mistakes, but Fortuna, the Roman goddess of chance, beloved of risk-takers and thrill-seekers everywhere, seemed to be behind the wheel. Also, there were always positive people along the way, cheering the whole thing along.

At first, Adam and I both thought this story had all started when he was driving back from his parents' house and saw an old double-decker bus abandoned in a field. The more we talked about it though, the more we realised that wasn't true. The bus wasn't the first time he'd had a laugh with vehicles or made a home out of a small space intended for other purposes. It wasn't the first time he'd run a business or built things either. Looking back, he'd served both official and unofficial apprenticeships.

On the Tools

Adam's been 'on the tools', working as a carpenter most of his life, partly because he didn't have much choice. He left school in 1987 with two CSEs, as they were called then, one in religious education and one in woodwork. It was pretty obvious he wasn't cut out for the cloth, so he chose woodwork. He'd been naturally good at that from the start, so much so that the bedside table he made for his final exam was paraded around his school like a crown and was allegedly the best thing anyone had ever made there. Having not turned up to most of his other lessons, he had little chance of passing anything like maths or English.

Ever since receiving his first 'Top of the Pops' drumkit for Christmas, aged eight, Adam had loved drumming. All he wanted to do when he left school was become a musician, but his dad Brian persuaded him to go to college, study carpentry and do an apprenticeship. He needed a sponsor for that, so he wrote to loads of local building companies. Some interviewed him, and one, Intec, decided to sponsor him. He'd attend college for a few weeks, then work on-site for Intec for a few weeks, initially as a dogsbody. He alternated like this for three years, on £28 per week pay.

His dad hoped he'd forget all about music but actually, as soon as he qualified as a carpenter, the very next day in fact, Adam handed in his notice.

Adam and his sister Nadia with Adam's first drumkit

He started looking for work as a drummer straight away, applying for positions advertised in the back of *Melody Maker*, the weekly music magazine that ran from 1926 to 2001. Musicians looking for others to join them would list bands they considered influences, then you'd turn up to audition, all optimistic, and find out they were nothing like those bands and it was all wishful thinking.

He went for quite a few auditions in London and ended up with a great psychedelic band called Walk on Water. His wife-to-be, Tanya, sang and my husband-to-be, Simon, played guitar. Aged 19, Adam moved into a shared house in London with the bass player, Flads. His carpentry, however, was crucial throughout that period because being a musician didn't earn him any money at all for ages.

Together with another musician-carpenter called Bill Woodruff, Adam started building rehearsal and recording studios, including Fortress Studios and Terminal Studios, where they were working between The Orb in one room and Motörhead playing 'Ace of Spades' in another. They built studios for artists too, like Incognito and Victoria Adams (later Beckham). From there, Adam moved on to doing general maintenance for Nomis Studios, where he found himself having Paul Weller play an acoustic version of 'That's Entertainment' for his ears only while he mended a floorboard – beautiful and moving, but awkward, since he needed to hammer nails and had to wait until Paul had finished so as not to seem rude.

Soon, Adam was doing maintenance work for billionaire philanthropist Lily Safra, who died in 2022. Known as The Gilded Lily, she had a house in Belgravia round the corner from her mate, Baroness Thatcher. Once, when Adam was due to go on holiday but was still half-way through some work in Lily's dressing room, he was summoned to her quarters, and the other staff were sure he was in trouble. In fact, while she expressed her displeasure, she also gave him an envelope, not to be opened until he was on his way home – it contained thousands of pounds' worth of spending money for his holiday. It's hard to spend that much on a long weekend going down the rapids at Center Parcs, but he did his best and appreciated the thought! Apparently, she was famously fond of giving extravagant gifts.

So, in short, Adam's trade has served him well, and buckling down for three years of his apprenticeship, especially when he was a bit of a loose cannon, remains the most sensible thing he's ever done. Fair play, Brian. Adam gets the last laugh though, because it enabled him to do far more daft projects later on than he would have managed otherwise, like converting unlikely things into homes; he could never have afforded to do that if he'd had to pay someone else to do the work.

Bangernomics and Car Trouble

Adam's love of vehicles started young. His favourite toy was a big plastic racing car you could sit on, push along with your feet and whizz around on. He loved it even once he'd outgrown it, so his agreement when his mum said they should give it away to some poor children was begrudging. She actually gave that, and many other toys, to a nursery in town, at which she later happened to enrol him.

He went there on the first day determined to make it work, but something wasn't right. There was a familiar air about the place. He started to spot all

Adam and his Triumph Dolomite

his beloved toys, and went round grabbing them from the other kids, saying 'That's mine!', furious that they'd stolen all his stuff for their own evil gain. The racing car was the last straw.

I suspect that day has something to do with his impulsiveness around vehicles, because Adam's had more wheels than he can remember, of every size from skateboards to diggers. There have been motorbikes and mopeds – Vespas, Yamahas and a Harley – as well as a buggy and a quad. Estate cars can carry a fair number of tools and drums, so he's had a couple of those, like an

Adam and Brian working on Adam's Triumph Dolomite

Alfa Romeo 159 and a Volvo 940. To cope with the muddy places he often ends up in, he's had a few 4×4s: Mitsubishis – a Pajero and an Outlander PHEV – and a Land Rover Defender. There've been a couple of saloons, like the BMW 5 and 3 Series, and several tiny, fierce superminis, like two Suzukis – one orange, one black – a Mini Clubman Cooper and a yellow Fiat Cinquecento.

In his twenties and thirties, Adam built up confidence with vehicles through his easy-come, easy-go attitude to car ownership. Nearly all new cars and most used ones are bought on finance of some kind rather than with cash. This allows you to buy something smarter than you can afford to buy outright, but it's a monthly drain on your budget and the value of the car often depreciates fast. He and our friends had a different approach in the nineties and beyond, inspired by not having steady jobs or enough money. UK motoring journalist James Rüppert, formerly a car dealer, published a great book called *Bangernomics* about this sort of approach, which I'd summarise as the science of running an old car for next to nothing. There's also a board game, a website, the *Bangerpedia* and informal get-togethers: check it out. Here's how it works.

Adam taking part in the Ace Cafe Brighton Burn Up &
Ride on his vintage 1980 hardtail Harley in about 2017

You buy a terrible old banger with a ton of character, which has somehow acquired a year's MOT, use it for a year until the MOT's due again and then, when it fails, scrap it and get another one. It works out much cheaper. Or pay a bit to keep it on the road another year if you prefer. Adam's cheapest was fifty quid from Mr Cheap Cars in Tooting. Simon got a few there too.

Before you have kids and need to be dependable, a bit of vehicular unreliability saves a lot of money. The best banger he ever got was a fabulous gold Ford Cortina that went for years – admittedly by buying unusually optimistic MOTs from Brixton. As a sensible(ish) grown-up, he bought a newer car a couple of years ago – a posh semi-electric thing for £23,000 from a dealer, but when he sold it a year and a half later he could only get £19,000 for it, so he lost four grand. Now, in the world of bangernomics, that buys you six years of cars!

Our circle also had a thing for classic cars, so when we went anywhere together it looked like *Wacky Races*. Simon had a Hillman Imp in California

Bronze, then a sexy green 1972 Reliant Scimitar, which he blew up showing off to me. I had a Ford Anglia like in the second Harry Potter book (but mine was two-tone black and white), our friends Bic and Chloe had an Anglia van, and another friend had an old taxi. Adam's cars tended to be slightly newer, like a fantastic tiny Suzuki SC100 Whizzkid we called 'The Egg', but he also went through a blue Triumph Dolomite, a black Chevrolet Corvette Stingray, a tan Austin Mini and the aforementioned Ford Cortina. None of these were terribly practical choices, but they were fun, and the smell of leaded four star and leatherette is still a nostalgia-triggering madeleine for us.

Being one of the smallest cars on the market, The Egg left something to be desired as a drummer's car, so Adam built a trailer for it. It was shaped like a wedge of cheese, painted black to match the car, and divided into foam-lined compartments for all the different drums, cymbals and hardware. He'd hook it to the back of The Egg whenever he needed to get his drums to rehearsals and gigs. He once went to collect his kit from the studio, only to find the place crawling with security, as Nirvana were rehearsing there before appearing at Reading Festival. Adam's kit was stored through the studio, so Nirvana had to wait while their security formed a human chain and helped Adam carry it all out and load it into the 'The Eggbox'.

Some of us were experimenting with living in vehicles even then. Our friend Julian converted an old van so he could sleep in it on walking holidays, Matthew lived in a vintage ambulance, and I co-owned a 1960s horsebox with a kitchen in the middle. Adam's idea, later on, of buying an old bus and making it into a home for himself and his daughter didn't seem any odder. That's what happens if you hang out with a bunch of enthusiasts and idealists.

Some of these ideas probably came from festivals; lots of us were regulars at Glastonbury and other smaller music events, before it was the hugely successful industry it is now in the UK, worth billions in 2023. Festivals made us all associate camping in tents and vans with fun, friends and a sense of freedom, not just rain and plaid thermos flasks of tomato soup like family camping holidays.

Messing About With Boats

Not all Adam's vehicles had wheels. One of the first boats he owned was a little one called a Microplus, moored on the River Medway in Tonbridge where his parents lived. Its name was *Daddy Cool II*, named after its predecessor, *Daddy Cool*. His partner at the time, Tanya, had a brother called Griff Fender who was in the doo-wop revival band Darts; they had a top-ten hit with the song 'Daddy Cool' in 1977, and this boat belonged to their proud dad. The single had more luck than the first boat named after it: a big wave caught *Daddy Cool* on her maiden launch in Worthing, and that was that.

Microplus made a variety of cool-looking fibreglass boats in the UK between the sixties and seventies. In the late nineties, Adam bought *Daddy Cool II* second hand with a trailer for tuppence ha'penny off Phil, who ran the boatyard, and he and Tanya did it up at weekends. They only slept in it once, which was very uncomfortable, but they used to go up and down the river and have a blast. They even used it to help a friend, Tim Brinkhurst, to film a river scene under Tower Bridge for his gangster movie *Gordon Bennett*, co-directed with Matthew Zajac.

In the film, a drug dealer offers to give up dealing if his girlfriend, decked out in a feather boa, gives up prostitution. She agrees, so he tips a sack of cocaine into the river. Budget constraints, environmental responsibility and the law being what they are, they used flour. Adam piloted the boat, ducking down to stay out of shot. This attracted the attention of the river police, who remonstrated with them but were persuaded to taste the flour and accept that they were not poisoning fish and would cause no further trouble.

That was fine until the boat ran out of petrol and Adam had to use the emergency dinghy oars to row himself to the bank. The tide was going out fast and he was nearly beached on the mud while waiting for a crew member to run to the petrol station and back for some fuel. Tides on the Thames are pretty hairy: fast and powerful. They were relieved when their friend got back just in time. He lowered the can to them and they managed to top up, start the engine and get away. They celebrated their close escape by mooring at a nautical-themed pub on a barge near Deptford called the Wibbly Wobbly, and stayed there until the tide reached the point at which they could use a slipway near Canary Wharf to get *Daddy Cool II* out of the water and back on the trailer after her adventure in the movies.

Daddy Cool II gave Adam and Tanya the bug for boats, so when Bluewater Shopping Centre in Dartford was new, they ran the pleasure boats on the little lake there. Phil, the owner of Tonbridge Waterway, had rowing boats at the lake, which shoppers could rent out to make the whole shopping thing less of a drag and more of a fun day out. It was quite a laugh at first, but like any job it had its irritations: people would never bring the boats back on time, and kids would lark about, picking up tons of their mates from the opposite shore, filling the boat with water. In the school holidays it got really busy with teenagers, bored of watching their parents shopping.

There was a boat enthusiast called Ian working with Tanya and Adam. He manned the bridge between the lakes, ready to call out if anyone had an accident, so that Adam could speed to the rescue in the world's most comically underpowered rescue boat. Ian left something to be desired as a watchman, as he was too boat-fixated to notice that kids were on the same little bridge as him, jumping off it behind his back.

Soon they sold the Microplus and bought another craft – a speedboat this time. They were living in London, so they moored the new boat at Kew, and sped up and down the Thames on her. A Dell Quay Dory she was – another British boat and allegedly an unsinkable whaler. They called her *DC3* (short for *Daddy Cool III*, but attempting to sound cooler). They used to thread their way through the city for a day trip, all the way to the Millennium Dome, which was finished by June 1999. Once Adam and Tanya were married in 1999, they focused on some more conventional things for a while, like raising their baby daughter, Devon.

Adam with baby Devon, born 2001 when Adam was 30

Vans and Vacations

As a carpenter and drummer, Adam Woods is a fine piece of evidence for nominative determinism (the theory that your name influences your career). He's not even the only carpenter-drummer called Woods that I know – there's also Melanie Woods, and even another Adam Woods in The Fixx, so that proves it. Anyway, vans big enough to carry materials, tools and drums help with both activities, so he's had a few in his time, including three or four VW surfer vans, a Renault Master, several Ford Transits, an LDV ex-Post Office van and Ford Escort vans originally used by the AA and Tonbridge Waterways. One of his favourites was a rear-engine VW T24 campervan in a brutal matt black. Devon and he converted that one when she was little. She wanted sparkly stars on the outside, so he mixed some gloss black paint with glitter, and then they made stencils together and covered it in constellations.

Tanya and Adam separated after a while and Devon ended up with her dad much of the time. He tried to work extra hard to earn money before her summer holidays so that he could be around when she wasn't at school, and she could choose an adventure. They'd find a way to make it work despite tight budgets – take the van on a ferry, or book flights and make the rest up as they went along. One year, she asked to go campervanning to the West Country in the VW 'starmobile'. They headed down to Cornwall, did pretty wild camping a lot of the time, and got hooked on surfing.

Another summer, she chose driving across Spain, so Adam sold his car, bought a dreadful old Wrangler left-hand-drive jeep, sailed from Portsmouth to Bilbao and they hit the road. The jeep was a wreck – really noisy and it kept breaking down. It wouldn't even start when Adam tried to drive it off the ferry, with everyone tutting and huffing in their cars behind them, waiting to start their holidays. It did alright in the end, getting them as far as Ibiza with the help of a few ferries.

It was a bit reckless, but it always worked out, whereas on the only occasion he booked a package holiday for the two of them it went horribly wrong. They headed off to Turkey for an all-inclusive fortnight, booked online. Once he'd booked, Adam realised that the transfer from the airport was about five hours, meaning they weren't going to the nearest airport. He complained and they changed it, but he trusted them less from then on, which led him to taking the unprecedented step of buying non-compulsory travel insurance – quite an alien concept for him. Maybe this insulted Fortuna, who usually seems to favour him.

All went well the first night and they had lovely seafood by the beach. The next morning, however, Adam felt weird and suggested a relaxing day by the pool rather than heading out exploring. It got worse and worse until he could barely cope with sunlight and was sweating so much that other holidaymakers were coming to ask if he was alright. It got so bad he had to ask one of the other parents to keep an eye on his very excited six-year-old daughter, who was having the time of her life, while he went back to the room to try to sleep it off. After a prolonged, distressing visit to the bathroom, he slept for hours. The helpful parents brought Devon up to the room and, shocked by the state of him, insisted he call down to reception for a doctor.

When the doc arrived, he ambulanced him to hospital with Devon, with Adam concentrating on not passing out on the way. They arrived at the hospital with no mobile phone, no insurance papers and no passports. Nurses hooked him up to drips and fed him a 'white diet' – pasta, rice, apple, and black tea with sugar – though he could barely eat any of it.

Day after day, he drifted in and out of consciousness while infant Devon found ways to fend for herself. Ingeniously, she pulled down the curtains to use as a blanket and slept on the sofa in the private room Adam found himself in. She scavenged from his uneaten pale food, and hung out by the vending machines, turning urchin and using any coins left behind to buy sweets.

The hospital refused to release Adam until they saw his documents, as the whole thing had cost a fortune, but he had no way of getting them. The state he was in, and the worry, made him so delirious that he became paranoid. He wanted to ask the nurses to stop putting him on drips, convinced they were poison, but he kept sleeping through the changeover of the bags and waking up with a full one. He lost touch with reality so badly that he barricaded the door with a sofa, wheeled the drip over to the third-floor window, climbed on a table and started yelling for help, saying they were poisoning him.

He was waving his arms, which meant the gravity-fed drip bag started filling with his blood. One look at his blood pumping into the clear fluid and your brave adventurer passed out and fell off the table. Hospital workers had to smash the door down to deal with the chaos. The next thing he knew, he was back in bed with a fresh bottle of drip.

The only phone number he knew by heart in these digital-dependent times was his parents'. From them he got Tanya's number, and stayed conscious long enough to explain the situation. He awoke to the sensation of someone touching his arm, and Tanya was there! Clearly, he was losing whole days to blackouts. She got Devon back to the hotel, retrieved Adam's documents, and managed to get him out just in time for their original flights back home. He'd spent 13 of their 14 holiday days in hospital. I think he got the message Fortuna! He went back to flying by the seat of his pants with luck (usually) on his side.

Downsizing in the Marina

Later, Adam bought a sailboat. Devon and he were living in a rented flat in Kemptown, Brighton, which he couldn't really afford. It was about £1,200 a month and he wasn't earning much as a carpenter, so he needed a solution.

He'd been reading Robin Knox-Johnston's book, *A World of My Own*, about going round the world single-handedly in the late sixties in the *Sunday Times* Golden Globe Race. The sailors involved in the race were using pretty basic kit, with no satellites of course, and they weren't allowed to stop anywhere. Knox-Johnston won, despite losing his self-steering gear off Australia. Adam was interested in the sailing but was more drawn to the solitary nature of the experience, and to how absorbing and engaging it was.

Knox-Johnston had to make sure he got enough exercise, and since there was terrible boredom en route, he had to make his own fun and excitement too, so he'd tie a line to the back of the boat and dive off the front, let the boat overtake him – a terrible risk in the middle of the Indian Ocean – then challenge himself to catch up with it, grab the line, pull himself aboard and do it all again. That borderline insanity caught Adam's imagination, and he thought, 'I could do that'. He planned to sell nearly all his stuff, put the rest in storage and live at Brighton marina on a sailing boat with Devon. He'd never sailed of course – he had no idea what he was doing, but, you know, how hard can it be?

He bought the boat on eBay and went to view it in Wisbech, on the borders of Cambridgeshire and Norfolk. An Invicta 24 called *Barbary*, she was a lovely old boat from the 1970s. Devon used to call her Barbara. The seller wanted to get shot of her quick before his divorce, or he'd have had to give half the proceeds to his ex. Adam told him the story – how his daughter and he wanted to live onboard in Brighton.

The seller seemed very taken with all this and asked Adam about his sailing experience. When he confessed he had none, the seller told Adam he was a nutcase, but he quite liked that. So he said, 'Well, how about this: instead of me giving half to my ex, I'll give half to you?' and sold it to him half-price. It's funny how, when you act on impulse and do things that are considered mad or unwise, other quite sensible people often join in too, as though they were just waiting for an excuse to throw their homework on the fire and take the car downtown. Many people who choose a conventional path themselves still like to help someone else along the road less travelled.

Barbary was delivered to Brighton and, after Adam had done the boat up, he and Devon lived onboard for about a year. She didn't need much work: he gave her a good clean and antifouled the hull to get rid of any seaweed, slime, kelp, sponges, sea squirts, worm casings, barnacles and mussels, and gave the deck a lick of paint. To make it more homely, he installed hanging pockets in Devon's bunk so she could keep her books, toys and colouring pens handy.

Barbary was a pretty fast racing boat. Adam and a friend Jack went out once and overtook loads of more modern boats, leaning over so far that the window at the head was underwater. However, she wasn't really suitable for living in – she was too small and narrow, and the marina isn't officially residential, so they had to keep it on the down-low. That said, quite a few people were up to the same thing at the time.

One day, Adam invited Simon on a trip across the channel. Simon's dad was an accredited skipper and Simon was Competent Crew, the new name for the Able Seaman qualification (because too many people made rude jokes about it, I suppose). Simon was full of enthusiasm at first.

'Great! Let's have a look at the charts.'

'Charts?'

'There are shipping lanes you know, Adam – some of the busiest ones in the world. It's like crossing a heaving, wet motorway. There are tankers and cargo ships piling through there. You need a passage plan and all sorts. Have you even got a radio?'

'No.'

Simon was appalled. He recommended they get themselves properly organised. To Adam, that all sounded sensible but a bit dull.

Not having received the answer he wanted, Adam talked to this old fella in a nearby mooring about it. He was an English guy with terminal cancer who had sailed all the way back from New Zealand to die closer to home. Adam explained he was a bit worried about sailing across the Channel but the old fella said just to get out and do it. He was probably pretty fatalistic, and not the best influence, but it was the push Adam was looking for.

So, he ignored Simon and went to France and back with the help of Google, another mate and a little luck, and had a lovely time. He read books and websites first of course – he doesn't have a death wish – but then he just had a go and was sold straight away. He made the crossing with Devon later, tying her to the mast like Ulysses so she wouldn't fall in. People watching through binoculars probably thought he was kidnapping her like a deranged pirate. It wasn't entirely safe, but don't worry, reader – she lived to tell the tale.

Spinning in the Solent

Even since the Big Green Bus, Adam's had a couple of sailing boats. One in, one out is his policy, not collecting. Not long ago, he and his partner Enfys bought a knackered 29-foot sailing boat for a grand. It was in a terrible state, so they did that up and sold it on for a profit, even after costs, which is an unusual thing in boating.

That convinced the two of them to pool resources and invest in 70 grand's worth of lovely, proper 40-foot sailing boat called *Westlin Winds*. It was named after a song by ladies' man and poet Robert Burns, about his beloved Peggy, who distracted him from his work. Apparently, she was 'a charming Fillette who lived next door to the school, overset my Trigonometry, and set me off on a tangent from the sphere of my studies.'

They thought it was a crap name, so they decided to give her a new one. Legend has it that every vessel is recorded by name in The Ledger of the Deep and is known to Poseidon, god of the sea. So, to change the name of a boat, you must first purge its name officially from the ledger and from Poseidon's memory. Turns out this is a bit of a faff.

The ritual begins with the removal or obliteration of every trace of the boat's current identity. Next, you write the old name on a metal tag in water-soluble ink. You will also be needing a bottle of Champagne. Addressing Poseidon verbally with great formality, you drop the tag in the water, pour in half the bottle of fizz, then tell Poseidon the new name, requesting safe passage. Pour in more champagne, then address the four winds by name – Boreas, Zephyrus, Eurus and Notus – flinging wine in each direction like a Formula 1 driver. If you have neither the time nor the budget for all that, you have to put up with a crap name, so they did.

They lived on *Westlin Winds* for a year, sailing around the Isle of Wight. The idea was to take her to the Mediterranean, but avoiding the Bay of Biscay, which is terrifying. You can sail to France, get a boatyard to take down the mast, and thread your way up the river Seine, through Paris. Then you join the canal system, popping out in the Med. The trouble was that it would have taken longer than they had because, after Brexit, they could only stay in the Eurozone for three months. Whichever way they looked at it, they couldn't get it done in time, as there's an 18-month limit on boat stays, after which time you have to pay a whopping tax. Even Adam admits that more research before starting would've been good on this occasion. It might have been better to buy a boat out there, but never mind. They sold *Westlin Winds* and made a profit again anyway.

Sailing's exhilarating but quite stressful because there are real dangers. You can't just switch off the engine and pull off to the side if things get sticky, so maybe Simon did have a point after all, especially since Adam lives with Ménière's disease (a rare inner ear condition that affects your balance and hearing). If he has an attack when sailing, that's pretty dangerous, as it leaves him completely incapacitated for a while.

He and Enfys had a couple of hair-raising moments caught in high winds in the Solent. *Westlin* had in-mast furling, meaning the sails tucked away inside the mast pole. When they bought the boat, they had to move it straight away to another mooring, so they headed out, and it quickly became clear that Enfys didn't fully know what she was doing. She let the sails out full in gusty winds, and the boat went right over. She was panicking and, although Adam managed to bring the boat round, she didn't know how to get the sails back in and there were lines everywhere.

Adam called to her to take the helm while he sorted it out, but she'd never done that either, so it turned out that she was on full lock while he was

Westlin Winds at sea

desperately trying to get the sails in as quickly as he could. He glanced up to see the Isle of Wight looming at them and heard Enfys crying and screaming, 'Someone help us!' When he looked up two seconds later, he could see England, so he realised with horror that they were spinning uncontrollably. It dawned on him that if he became ill it would be very serious. They motored to the marina after that.

Adam and Salbo aboard *Westlin Winds*

Inventions and Experiments

The bus and cabin weren't Adam's first business ventures. He's always fizzed with ideas for new products and services. If you try enough things, something might work, or you might have fun failing.

Adam's then-business partner, Philippa, and he even took something on *Dragons' Den* once. Philippa did the presentation for their product, Spot On: spring-loaded, coloured shades you could apply to ceiling-mounted spotlights to change the ambience of any room. She had the idea, then Adam designed the mechanism using coat hangers and got a prototype made up. They stoked some interest at the Ideal Home Exhibition with Spot On, but it never really took off, that idea.

He got further with 'It's-ezibay', a business run by friends Jon, Louise, Karron and himself. They offered a service that listed your possessions for you on eBay in return for a commission. They'd take care of the photography, description and fees, then forward you your money when your item sold. With the catchy slogan 'turn your trash into cash' it worked very well but was ezi to copy, so someone did. They ran it for eight months or so and collected some very unusual items, including an allegedly 'as-new' sex swing from a woman in Worthing.

He also had a couple of great straw-related ideas. Firstly, and he stands by this one, advertising on straws, printed with non-toxic ink. Think about it – you bring it up close to your face already, so you could read something printed on it, like the jokes on ice lolly sticks. You could target your audience pretty accurately, advertising products likely to appeal to drinkers of boba tea on fat straws, printing clubber-friendly ads in UV-fluorescent ink for nightclub cocktails and pushing health products to drinkers of raw kale and ginger smoothies.

The second straw-related idea is so good it's now been done. As a lover of ramen, Adam found the spoon got in the way while using the chopsticks and you end up with a soupy tabletop, so he thought, what if the chopsticks were hollow? They'd be multifunctional: pick up the veg, suck up the soup, all without mess. He explained this to a waiter at the Chinese restaurant opposite The Dublin Castle in Camden while he was waiting to play a gig. He agreed it was a good idea and left Adam to gloat over his imminent fortune while enjoying their wonderful speciality, sticky Marmite squid.

Adam went back six months later and ordered the ramen. Guess what cutlery it came with? Chopstick straws. He didn't see the waiter, who was probably on his superyacht in Monaco. The restaurant's closed down now, but whether that's because karma got the better of them or because they're too busy selling millions of his invention, Adam doesn't know. He just misses the squid.

Adam's most risqué venture, a hit with Brighton hipsters, was called Porniture. He upcycled cheap, old, junk shop furniture with decoupage, glueing coloured cut-outs all over it and sealing with varnish. The images he chose were kitsch, dated, soft-pornographic photographs from fruity seventies magazines that he found amusing. Some of the items looked pretty great. He even took a few commissions, including a piano decorated with a niche set of images requested by a gay couple. The people who run the Venustempel sex museum in Amsterdam bought one of his chests of drawers, and he believes it is still in service to exhibit the history of phallic sexual aids.

- 2 -
Surfing and Stableyards
Starting the Big Green Bus adventure

Surf Shack

The adventure of the Big Green Bus started in earnest when, on his way home from visiting his parents, Adam noticed an old bus rotting in a field. It was an old Routemaster. For anyone reading who isn't from the seventies like Adam and me, or a bus nerd, those are the buses that were open at the back so you could hop on and off at will – before we had health and safety. You'd pay your fare to a conductor with a ticket machine round his neck or, if you were feeling naughty, hop off before he came downstairs.

There's something appealing about big vehicles, isn't there? It starts at a young age. Generations of kids have learned to love vans like *Scooby Doo*'s Mystery Machine, trains like Thomas and Ivor, and weird stuff like Thunderbirds and Transformers. Nothing's really changed: kids today still love playing with big vehicles – toy trucks, trains, fire engines, diggers... and buses. Adam says he just never grew up.

Anyway, he pulled over and went and had a look at this bus. It was a knackered old wreck, irretrievably stuck in the mud. Nevertheless, it gave him an idea and, when he got home, he decided to have a look and see how much buses sold for. A quick poke around online showed him something interesting: double-decker buses are cheap. Perhaps he should have been suspicious at that point and wondered why, but no. Instead, he thought, 'Everyone else is missing a trick here. I could convert one of these. We could stay in it, me and Devon, in Cornwall. A holiday home for surfing breaks: happy days!'

Obviously that was a bonkers idea, especially as there's probably a law against living in Cornwall if you're called Devon. They'd at least have force-fed her jam-first scones. It would never have worked. But without that idea he'd never have ended up where he did, powered by blind enthusiasm, and he wouldn't have wanted to miss it. Hop on and I'll tell you the story.

Bus hunting

The only research he did was a round trip to Brighton on a double-decker. Obsessive vehicle owner that he is, Adam hadn't used public transport for years, so he sat on the top deck all the way to Brighton, and moved downstairs for the return trip. He spent the journey just looking around, visualising where everything would go in a conversion.

It didn't take long to find someone online who sold buses. His favourite prospect was a bus dealer called Mike up in the Midlands somewhere. He had loads of buses, Mike. Adam didn't really know what he was doing, what he was looking for. He only had two criteria: one was that he wanted a bus with the engine in the rear, because of the ideas he had brewing about layout. The other was that he needed it to run, as he had to drive it back to Brighton or he'd have to waste loads of money on transport, which is annoying when what you're buying is transport.

Normally, you need to pass the PCV (passenger carrying vehicle) Category D test to drive a bus. However, there was a loophole: if you had a full Category B (car) driving license, were over 21 and had been driving for at least two years, you could drive a bus made more than 30 years before the date it was being driven, if it wasn't being used for business purposes or for carrying more than eight passengers. Basically, that meant he could drive an old double-decker without taking a special test, so long as he didn't fill it with people or start selling tickets.

It was early 2013, so the youngest bus he could get would be from 1983. He chose a 1982 MCW Metrobus from Coventry, registration NOA 464X, with a bullet-proof ten-litre Gardner diesel engine at the back, without knowing any more than that it ran. I say 'chose' but, let's be honest, it was the first eligible bus he saw, which is how he tends to go about things. Adam's philosophy is that if you think about things too long, you end up thinking yourself out of them. Then your life's one adventure shorter than it could have been. You've got a small window of opportunity to do offbeat things and after that you start doubting yourself and you don't do it.

This approach can backfire, obviously. Neither of us is recommending you live your whole life like that, or on the roll of a die. Had he done more research than sitting on a bus, he'd have discovered that buses are cheap because you can't put them anywhere and they're a pain. Still, once he'd agreed to buy the bus he had to make it happen, so he did.

Speaking of which, he needed to get some money in order to pay for it, since he had none. The only thing he had of any value was his van, a white VW T5 which he loved, but he needed money for the project, so it had to go. Some people wouldn't sell a useful thing they have and like on the strength of a whim, but Adam did. The ten grand he got for it set the budget for Project Bus.

There was one tiny flaw in this plan. Unfortunately, he still needed money to live on and his only income was from carpentry; that meant he needed a van, so part of that cash had to be used immediately to buy another one. He bought a bangernomics old Post Office van for about 250 quid to get backwards and forwards from Brighton to the bus and carry tools about. Problem solved.

On a cold, frosty day, Devon and he took a day trip to the Midlands to have a look at the Metrobus, which was parked on a drab industrial estate with potholed roads. Mike had parked the bus on the road outside the lot and told them to go and have a look at it while they waited for him to arrive. A bus is open all the time – you just press the concertina door and it opens up, so they had a good poke around.

Everything about it brought back memories: the smell, the shapes, the seats. It reminded Adam of the lovely old green bus he used to take to school when he was a kid in Tonbridge. He hated school, partly due to undiagnosed dyslexia. In the year he should have been studying for his 11 plus, he spent most of the time litter-picking on the playing fields. His reading difficulties meant teachers assumed he was incapable of learning, and they couldn't think of anything else for him to do. That didn't set him up well for secondary school, where he became a shy but naughty teenager, smoking fags at the back of the bus, hiding behind his fringe and fantasising about Zoe, a girl he was too scared to talk to.

Showing early entrepreneurial skill, he spent the canteen money his mum gave him on KitKat six-packs which he sold as singles for 20 pence a pop to other kids on the bus, making a cool 50 pence profit, enough to buy some chips and a little extra for hiding away in his bedroom. He'd use this stash to buy fags or, with his mate Callum, to buy a bumper bottle of Cinzano if they had a party to go to. They'd get a bottle of lemonade too, tip half out, top it up with Cinzano and hide it in a bush to pick up on the way to the party. The Big Green Bus wouldn't be the first time he'd made enough money from buses to finance a glamorous lifestyle!

This bus was an MCW, which stands for Metro Cammell Weymann, a British bus manufacturer and bus-body builder based at Washwood Heath in Birmingham. Devon and Adam took lots of photos and fell in love with it a little. It seemed a shame to rip the interior out really. He worried bus spotters would be angry about his desecration of the bus as there aren't many of these left, but they've been very positive, feeling it'd been saved from the crusher. Besides, nothing was wasted; he sold off any surplus parts.

When Mike arrived, Adam bluffed his way through a discussion about engine matters neither knowing what he was talking about nor understanding what Mike was saying. Mike could've said anything to him, as long as the engine worked.

It was test drive time. Adam drove while Mike told him what to do. It was pretty straightforward, with an automatic three-speed gearbox. Because you sit quite low in the front, as low as you are in a small van, it doesn't feel like you're driving a bus. It's only when you look in the rearview mirror that you realise you've got a massive hunk of metal following you about. They drove around the industrial estate; Adam reversed the bus round a corner, and Mike said he was a natural. That bit of flattery was enough to make Adam part with four and a half grand! Well played, Mike.

So that was that: the die was cast. They couldn't take the bus home that day but Adam bought it and arranged to pick it up. Before he could do that, he had to find a place to put it while he converted it from defunct bus to mobile surf shack.

Devon on the upper deck of the bus before conversion

Adam drives the bus

Local Paper Saves the Day

This is when Adam discovered one of the reasons why double-decker buses in particular are so cheap to buy: it's because you can't put them anywhere – they're way too massive. He needed to find a plot of land or a yard that the bus could be parked on while he did the conversion work. He figured it would take him six to eight months to convert it, working on it full time, but knew it could be longer. There was no particular rush – he was just doing it for himself and Devon.

The ideal workshop site would have been somewhere warm, or at least under cover with electricity, but the budget didn't stretch to such luxuries. In fact, despite looking in the local paper, searching online, and asking local friends and contacts, he couldn't find anywhere to put it. Getting desperate, he tweeted 'Does anyone have any land near Brighton I could put this bus on while I convert it into a camper?'

From that, local paper *The Argus* got hold of it and ran a little story on a particularly slow news day: 'Man buys bus'. They sustained their interest in Adam and the bus for years, running stories like 'Sussex's bus-iest holiday getaway' and 'The best staycations to enjoy without leaving Sussex', which was a great help. When a local junior school approached him about helping

The bus before conversion, at the stableyard

them to convert a double-decker into a science classroom, *The Argus* even wrote 'Bus holiday pioneer to help school with science project'.

Also through *The Argus*, he finally found a place to put the bus: a stableyard just outside Brighton. There was no power, which meant he had to buy a generator to run the power tools, but all that worked out fine. The owner was a pragmatic lady who let him use a corner of the site and get on with the work for a year at the rate of a hundred quid a month, which seemed very reasonable.

Meanwhile, in London... someone sitting at a desk in the office of Plum Pictures, award-winning producers of factual television, was tasked with casting a series called *George Clarke's Amazing Spaces*, which was to be shown on Channel 4. It's a BAFTA-nominated makeover show that's proved madly popular internationally and celebrated its 10th anniversary in 2023. The first series had already aired, and they were about to film the second one.

They were looking for people turning unconventional things into places to live, with a particular emphasis on fun, creative use of small spaces, like vehicles. They wanted dramatic conversions to make the series more exciting, and they especially fancied a double-decker bus. Stumbling on 'Man buys bus' in *The Argus* online, they changed the next decade of Adam's life. I guess the lesson here is 'support your local paper'.

Mr Plum, smoking a huge cigar, called Adam and said he was gonna make him a star. Well, not quite, and there isn't a Mr Plum, but someone did call and say, 'Do you wanna be on TV?' and he thought, 'Ooh, OK!' expecting there'd be a ton of money, which was in short supply at the time, but he was wrong there. There was no pay for the TV show, although it took a load of time and effort and caused delays in the work. Adam still saw the bus as a personal project at that stage, not a business, but why say no to a new opportunity?

Someone advised him that with TV companies you have to wait till they've done some filming of you, invested some time, before you ask for anything much, but at that point they're sometimes more committed and can be more flexible. Adam signed the contract – a one-sided thing it was, saying they had loads of rights and Adam had responsibilities, and they may or may not even end up using him.

All of a sudden, it got a bit real. Adam realised that, because he'd be filmed doing this, and was still running a business doing carpentry and relying on that for his livelihood, it could get pretty embarrassing if he messed it up. Better not mess it up then, he thought.

Drive-by Shooting

Because they like to narrate all the important stages of a makeover-format story, Plum Pictures wanted to film Adam bringing the bus back to Brighton from the Midlands. He took a train to Plum's offices in Camden, and from there he got in a car with a cameraman, the director and the producer for their road trip to Coventry.

Mike had agreed to meet them halfway from his yard, at a service station. The plan was that he'd drive the bus all the way to Brighton, but somewhere in the middle they'd pull over and the crew would film Adam driving it briefly. Mike would take over and drive the rest of the way to Brighton train station, where Adam would pay his fare home and drive the bus down the road to the stableyard. You'll have gathered by now that Adam's not the most cautious man, but even he started to get a bit nervous about driving this massive thing. He consoled himself with the fact that at least he wouldn't have to get it all the way to the coast himself – that would be terrifying.

Adam was petrified of going under any really low bridges. Many bridges in the UK are set higher than a double-decker bus, or buses are built to be lower than many (but not all) bridges. It's even worse in Europe, where the bridges are much lower, possibly because they tend to have only single-deckers. Until 2021, when bridge-alert technology was rolled out nationwide, double-deckers regularly crashed into the 18,000 low bridges across the UK. It's not good for the buses: they come back as open-tops, if they come back at all.

Still in London, Plum took forever getting all their gear in the car. Adam kept checking the time as it got later and later. At last, they hit the road. Mike and the bus were still at the service station when they arrived, but they were so, so late that plans had to change. It was going to be too late for Mike to get home by train by the time he'd driven all the way to Brighton. Being a pragmatic, problem-solving kind of guy he said, 'Look, why don't I just give you a quick lesson around this service station car park, Adam, and then you can go back on your own with the TV crew?' Adam wasn't convinced: he'd driven plenty of vans, and the crew had come all this way, but he really wasn't feeling confident about driving a 14-ton aluminium box all the way back to Brighton.

The thing is, adventures tend to lack a reverse gear; you can only really move forwards once you've begun the journey. In the words of Heyload (Bent but not Broken) in the forum of the Adventure Rider website for motorcycle riders, 'There is no reverse because as ADV riders, we do not retreat. FORWARD, TO ADVENTURE!!!!' In this spirit, Adam agreed to Mike's suggestion, and Plum mounted little GoPro cameras on the windscreen of the bus. They also had a big camera in their car, pointing backwards; they kept overtaking and filming Adam as he was driving down the motorway. The bus was particularly slow because this was a city bus, not a long-distance coach. It only had three gears so it really couldn't manage more than 40 miles per hour, this brick pushing through the air. It lumbered along in the slow lane, overtaken by even the slowest lorries.

If the pressure wasn't enough that Adam had to drive, he had to do it while being filmed. The Plum car kept speeding ahead and looking down on him from bridges to film the bus driving underneath, while he was trying to focus so as not to crash; it was like a race against the paparazzi in slo-mo. He had to keep reminding himself this wasn't a short van but a long bus, especially when they got onto smaller, twistier roads.

He enjoyed it after a while, but it took a long, long time to get back. Mike was right: they didn't reach Brighton till it was nearly dark. They stopped for a cuppa half-way, where Adam got a kick out of parking with his fellow coaches like a proper PCV driver, which was some consolation.

Salbo

One crucial addition to the family at this point was Salbo. Devon had been begging for a dog with stubborn regularity for literally years. When she was very young, Adam managed to fob her off with a couple of goldfish called Goldie and Charlotte, but Charlotte promptly died. He suggested they wrap her up, pop her in the freezer, then bury the two fish together when Goldie died... he didn't think they'd be waiting long.

Adam tried his best to organise healthy meals but, as for any single parent, life was busy: managing work, laundry, drop-offs, packed lunches, pick-ups and dinner could be a lot of balls to juggle. One morning, he grabbed a couple of frozen salmon fillets to defrost in the fridge ready for dinnertime. When they got home in the evening, the whole flat stank, and they found he'd defrosted one fillet, and one Charlotte. They had to flush her down the loo in the end, so the reunion in a shared crypt never came to pass. Goldie kept going for years, moving from house to house with them.

With Devon still pushing hard for a dog, Adam compromised, with a cat. Their one-eyed cat came from the local RSPCA and was named after Gordon Brown. Gordon was looked after by adoring elderly neighbours Baz and Chaz while Devon and Adam went to Glastonbury Festival one year. Sadly, Gordon died before they got home, so Baz and Chaz dutifully buried him in the back garden. Being a little frail, they hadn't dug deep enough, so Adam and Devon returned to find that foxes had exhumed Gordon and left him on the grass. Adam dug a deeper hole and laid Gordon to rest, but foxes aren't stupid and they disinterred him again a couple of days later. It got so frequent that Devon used to get home from school and call out 'Da-ad. Gordon's been dug up again!' It didn't matter how deep he dug, the foxes would outsmart him.

Ground down enough by this to bow to the inevitable dog, they went to the Dogs Trust, where they found Sally, known as Salbo. She is a very beautiful, if rather mournful-looking, border collie–husky cross from Ireland. They love that hairy, stinky mutt. She never leaves Adam's side if she can help it: she's kept him company during the build, run with him every other day, and is a big hit with viewers and followers on social media. She's also lent him her ears more and more as his hearing has deteriorated, alerting him to arrivals and to danger. So yes, Devon, he's admitted it: you were right. What your household and the bus needed was a dog – this dog.

Salbo at the seaside

- 3 -
Skip-Diving and Selling Seats
Building the Bus from Top to Bottom

Before the 'Before'

Adam got the bus safely home to its temporary stableyard, but then he wasn't allowed to do anything to it. The work couldn't begin until Plum had brought presenter George Clarke along for the initial, 'So what have you bought and what's the plan?' interview. Nothing could be done to the bus till then, because they needed to film it in all its crumbling, filthy, neglected glory to emphasise the transformation later. TV, it turned out, was full of these contrasts – one day it's all go, go, go with crew, equipment, arrangements and presenters, then it's wait, wait, wait.

Adam used the time to sit down and work out how he was going to do it. He planned more carefully than he would have done otherwise, so the delay was a blessing in disguise. Since the idea was to stay in the bus himself with Devon, it didn't need to be fancy. Having spent four-and-a-half of his ten grand buying the bloody thing, there wasn't much of a budget. The five-and-a-bit left after buying a replacement van clearly wasn't going to be enough, but it would go further if it was thought through in advance. He spent quite a while measuring, sitting in different parts of the upper deck, costing out materials and settling on a plan.

Still thinking it would be an overgrown campervan that would be safe to drive on the highway, his work converting boats had taught him that he needed to consider weight distribution carefully. Anything heavy had to be downstairs to make the bus more stable, especially for the rare occasions he'd have to drive it. What's more, the weight had to be evenly distributed, for cornering stability. If he put it all on one side, the bus could end up on top of several flat pedestrians.

He calculated that the beds could be built-in quite lightly, so he decided to give them a bedroom each upstairs, aiming for two double rooms with a narrow corridor down one side. For visitors, he worked out that a couple of single bunks could be squeezed in as well, right at the back. The space left at the front was too small for a room, and a wall would have made the corridor dark, so he kept in a couple of the original seats to make a nice, bright landing with a reading area.

Adam and Devon had learned from living aboard *Barbary* that, when you're living in a snug space with other people, it's good to be able to get some privacy now and again. For the bedrooms to feel private, they needed doors that could be closed. This was a problem though: the rooms were so small that if the doors swung open inwards there'd be no space at all and it would feel very cramped; if they swung outwards they'd hit people walking down the corridor, and anyway the corridor was too narrow, with a low ceiling that sloped down to the windows at the edge of the bus. Any door would have to be rather slender and curved, with a corresponding curved door frame to close into. He thought about having sliding doors that tucked inside the room, but that wasn't possible as space constraints meant he had to build the beds right up to the wall.

It was a relief when he had a light bulb moment and decided to create pocket doors. These are sliding doors that disappear nattily into a compartment in the wall when they're open. They're either hung from an overhead track or mounted on tracks or guides fixed to the floor. He'd seen these on sites where he'd worked, and been impressed, but had never installed one, so he'd have to work out how to do it.

On the top deck, if you looked from the front window towards the back of the bus, there was a stairway to the left, with a balustrade wrapping behind it to protect passengers from tumbling down the hole. That was the furthest point forward that he could site the front bedroom wall, so he placed it there to make the rooms as big as possible. The access corridor would be on the right, along by the windows.

To decide where to site the boundary wall between the first and second bedrooms, he needed to leave room to fit a regular double bed in each: four-and-a-half feet wide by about six-and-a-half feet long – plus a little space to enter and turn around, about 18 inches wide. There would be no room for a wardrobe or chest of drawers, unfortunately. He decided the cheapest, most space-efficient way to do it was to buy hinged bed frames – the ones designed to let you lift the base easily to store clothes and bedding underneath. He managed to source a couple of these second-hand.

He wanted the dividing wall between the bedrooms to be directly above the log burner, so that the flue could rise up between them, in fireproof boxing. His cunning plan was to install vents to either side that could be opened, one into each bedroom, to give them basic central heating in the winter.

Each bedroom needed to have a whole window, he felt, which limited the options for where the walls could go, as each pane was so wide. He also needed to remove some of the windows, to create privacy and warm the space up by allowing him to insulate the exterior walls. The plan was to use cut sheet aluminium attached to the outside to blank off the gaps left by missing windows, then add insulation and board them over with wood on the inside.

On the day George came to see the bus it was rainy and grim, and the yard was a mud puddle. The Plum people were happy because that's what you want on a 'before' shoot. Adam showed George around the inside, and George pointed out that the windows all leaked. They inspected the thick rubber seals around the edges. The bus was made in 1982 and over the decades these seals had filled up with grit and dirt from the roadside. They had expanded each winter when the water inside them froze, then contracted as it thawed in summer. In the moist shade, moss had grown all the way around the inner perimeter. The rubber had perished over time too, and the combination had left the seals porous. Through capillary action, the water from outside the window gets sucked inside, sinks into the moss and dirt, and then slowly drips all over everything.

Adam showed George plans and talked him through them as they poked around the bus. The idea was that he'd stick to these plans. What actually happened was that he lost them and ended up doing something a little different. It's all in his head, you see, but that usually works alright if you're doing it all by yourself.

Power and Ponies

There were three problems to work around with the site Adam was renting. The first was emotional: he didn't feel welcome. The owner was always fine with him, but her daughters seemed disapproving about the whole business. Every month he'd go round to the tack room and pay his dues to an unsmiling daughter among the crops and saddles. They couldn't wait to get rid of him after 12 months, to the day.

It was a different world, and he didn't fit in at all. This feeling was exacerbated every weekend, when the place would fill up with trailers, horseboxes and big cars. The equestrian community of Sussex would spill out of the vehicles, all completely ignoring him. Not one of them spoke to him in a year, which was quite surreal and alienating; it made Adam feel like a noisy ghost.

Problem number two was the geography of the site: it was open to the elements, which wasn't ideal. Extreme weather made this especially hard, since mean temperatures in March 2013 were 2.2°C, their lowest for 130 years and the second coldest ever recorded. Also, it wasn't flat and so the bus had to be parked on a slight incline – just enough to mean that he couldn't use a spirit level for any part of the build. That was a bit of a head-scratcher. To make sure doorways and all the other woodwork were in line with one another, but not with the sloping ground, he had to create a datum line. This is how they measured before the invention of spirit levels. It takes a while to get this absolutely right, and if you don't, nothing fits together properly or looks good.

To create the datum line, he took tons of measurements to find the dead centre of the bus from every boundary – top to bottom, side to side, front to back. He then used a permanent marker and a straight edge to draw a vertical line climbing up the middle of the windscreen, Spider-Manning back along the ceiling separating right from left, dropping down the centre of the back window, to the floor and crawling forwards along the centre aisle, all the way to the front, on both decks. Every measurement Adam took for the rest of the build would come off that loop, so he couldn't go far wrong. If anything was a little off, it would at least all be off in the same way. Nowadays, you can get laser levels and adjust them according to your datum line, but Adam didn't have one in 2013.

The third problem was the lack of services: water and especially power, which is tricky if you have to use electrical tools. He researched generators and found that Hondas were considered the best. The trouble was, they weren't affordable on his budget, so he got a cheaper version which worked for a couple of months then gave up. Fellow generator owners on an internet forum helped him to work out what was wrong. The problem involved an internal switch, and the price of replacement and repair would have been more than a new machine, so he had to scrap that one, unfortunately. Reluctant to risk another new generator burning out after a couple of months, he managed to find a second-hand Honda, which was brilliant. You live and learn. Feel free to send him a generator in return for this endorsement, Mr/Mrs Honda.

Standing Room Only

At last, the planning period was over; it was time to get his head down and make a start. While the cameras were rolling, he got the angle grinder out and removed a couple of the seats with George's help. Once the film crew had gone, he kept working, taking out all the upstairs seats. Many years of working in houses and doing carpentry had taught him to start at the top and work down, to avoid damaging the freshly decorated area by carrying materials through it, so the plan was to nearly finish upstairs first. It was spring, but since it still felt like the depths of winter, with snow and storms, he took out all the downstairs seats too and stored most of them under a tarpaulin outside. This left the lower deck clear as a storage area for materials, to keep them dry, and as a workshop protected from the elements to cut the wood. Setting up a sheet of thick plywood on a couple of trestles as his rudimentary workbench, he got stuck in.

All the air ducting that had run along the bottom of the walls to heat the seats and the passengers – he took all that out too. He even took down the inner ceiling because double-deckers aren't usually insulated – there's just a thin aluminium outer skin with aluminium struts to support it, then another inner skin of aluminium, even thinner, coated in white laminate, with nothing in between. To allow him to insulate the roof properly to keep the bus warmer, the inner layer came down. His plan was to add a thick layer of insulation, then board up the ceiling again.

Once the upper deck was empty, he was surprised by the size of it. It was quite an inspiring blank canvas. It was straightforward to build the dividing

The upstairs corridor, with the bunks at the back and bedrooms to the left

walls, except that the first-fix electrics had to be installed at the same time – pulling through all the cables to the locations of the various sockets and lights. A friend of his, Rod, came down from Birmingham to help him. They used a special fire-resistant cable, which had a good, thick protective covering. This was a bit of an investment but they didn't want to risk it getting rubbed and shorting out on the aluminium chassis if the bus ended up being driven around a lot. Adam had to think about the exact location of every socket and switch at this early stage, which was difficult but it worked out alright; after all, he'd converted and built many things before. When I had to specify locations for every socket and switch for the first time while getting a house rewired in the same year, I was so clueless that I only planned for half the number I should have and a friend mocked, 'When are you getting this rewired? The 1980s?'

The beds had to go into the rooms before Adam finished the inner walls so that he could box them in. He used second-hand insulation in the internal

A London Transport-themed bedroom on the bus

walls, then tongue-and-groove timber for the inner skin, to add a bit of visual decoration and tactile appeal. This layer helped to ensure the heat from the log burner would heat the bedrooms, not escape into the corridor with its wall of chilly windows. As anyone who's sat in a traffic jam in a pre-aircon old banger knows, metal boxes pass on excess heat in the summer as well as cold in winter, but the insulation helped to regulate the temperature either way.

The studwork – the supporting framework for the walls – was easy to erect, but when it came to the tongue-and-groove lining, Adam started off with green, water-resistant, beaded MDF sheets that had tongue-and-groove marks routed into them, rather than using individual lengths of timber. He thought that would be easier, but actually, when it came to scribing around the curved surfaces as they taper inwards at the top of the wall, measurements were tricky.

He decided to take special care to measure one sheet perfectly, then use that as a pattern to cut all the others. It took a long time, as scribing is a bit of an art – you cut the piece of wood slightly larger than you need, use a pencil to draw around the awkward, irregular area you're fitting it to, then use a jigsaw to get a neat fit. After scribing the first sheet carefully, Adam was so chuffed with the match that he got carried away and fitted it, without drawing round it as a template. After staring lovingly at his masterpiece, he realised he'd used up his template, swore, and started all over again. Repeatedly.

The interior walls crossed some of the windows, and he didn't want the untidy cross-section of the wall to be visible from outside the bus with all its cables and insulation showing, so the plan was to take some windows out when Plum next came to film – four upstairs and two downstairs. His intention was to get the panes out carefully in one piece and store them safely in case he ever needed a spare.

On the day of filming, Plum set up the shot and Adam started with one of the downstairs windows, working along the rubber seal, trying to ease out the pane. Having not really thought it through though, when his efforts failed with the cameras rolling, he got overexcited, grabbed a hammer and smashed it in, thinking it would be good telly. He did end up needing a spare, of course, but had to buy one instead.

Once the unwanted windows were out, one way or another, he had blank panels professionally cut from aluminium, which was pretty pricey. Using mastic to hold them in place, he then attached them properly with self-tapping screws, to withstand wind and weather. Once he'd painted the bus, they looked smart, the joins almost invisible.

He didn't just want to take windows out though, he wanted to put some in too, between the bedrooms and corridor. Depending on where the bus was parked, there might only be sunlight from one side, and the plan was to move the bus around a lot, so he wanted to borrow light from either side of the bedroom walls by installing internal windows. He had to make sure the pocket doors, cables and switches weren't in the way of these windows.

For the pocket doors, he settled on a wardrobe sliding door mechanism, routing out the studwork plate at the bottom, so that the 18 mm door slid into the rebate. The doors were full height and slid neatly into the bedroom wall when open, between the inner and outer skins: very satisfying. They saved loads of space and worked without a hitch for ten years. George Clarke seemed very taken with them. Once the walls were all formed and the beds and doors were in, he insulated the roof and lined it, so heat wouldn't be lost upwards.

Next, he built bunks across the very back of the bus. They crossed the rear fire exit, which is the back window, so the top bunk had to be positioned to make sure the fire escape was still usable. The bunks were quite small, so the mattresses had to be specially made. What Adam didn't foresee was what an awkward and hideous job it would be making and stripping those beds over the next decade, but visiting kids loved them. It was like a little den with a ladder, socket and light, and two cosy beds.

Publicity and Pace

Plum Pictures would visit to film specific jobs, such as the removal of the windows, wall building and insulation, to create a makeover montage. Then they'd disappear for ages until something else was due to happen that they thought was visually interesting or important for the narrative. They always coyly gave themselves a Get Out of Jail Free card, saying, 'It might not be a feature in the main programme – it may just be a little sideline thing', but as things progressed it became pretty obvious it would be one of the main features, because of how much time and money they were putting into the filming.

Adam got used to the fact that, when they visited, it was hard to make progress. They'd ask him to screw something in, take it out, try again from another angle, look at the camera this time, don't look at the camera this time, do it more slowly, over and over. Over five or six visits, it slowed him down quite a bit, but he felt it was well worth it. Having the extra accountability helped him to keep the quality high and made him start to think of the project in a more business-minded way. He focused on the finish more than he might have done for a private project, because it was going to be scrutinised, and he didn't want to look an idiot.

Having Plum Pictures involved trained him to be more publicity conscious too. Adam started blogging about his progress and found that there was a lot of interest online. He played it by ear, seeing what worked, trying to encourage people to like, comment on and share posts. He'd tell people about the ups, like completed stages of the build, and the downs, like massive holes in the floor. He'd post a photo of a lottery ticket he'd bought, and ask, 'Who wants some money? Comment, like and share if you want to split the winnings. Fingers crossed!' He'd encourage people to 'spot the dog' by taking shots of the bus site with Salbo behind a bush somewhere.

Another good thing about having TV involved was that it made sure he'd keep the pace up and finish the project. It could easily have dragged on and taken ages otherwise. He gave it as much time as possible, dropping Devon, in her first year of secondary school, off at breakfast club at school at half seven. She'd have after-school club as well, so he wouldn't get her till half five. That gave him all the time in the middle; sometimes in the summer, when the daylight lasted longer, he'd pick her up and bring her down to the bus for a couple of hours in the evening while he finished off. Devon had some creative input too: she made the collage of surf pictures in the stairway, which was a great feature, inspired by their plans to use the bus for surfing holidays.

Cops and Robbers

Part way through the work, Adam woke up one morning, went to take Devon to school but found no van. The cheap little Post Office van he'd bought at the start of the project to get backwards and forwards between Brighton and the bus and to carry tools about had disappeared. It hadn't cost much but the lack of a vehicle left him stuck. It wasn't the end of the world, and he hadn't liked it anyway, so didn't really care, except that he'd have to pay to replace it. The loss of all the tools was a different matter. This was a serious and immediate problem. They were worth thousands, he needed them to earn money as well as for the build, and couldn't afford to replace them. The whole project suddenly looked impossible.

About an hour later though, the cops saved the day, arriving in a police van with most of his tools. This included a Festool plunge saw that was worth about twice as much as the van. Adam was seriously relieved and could hardly believe the thieves had left all this by the side of the road instead of selling it. Some things were gone for good, though. A big box of hand tools including old things his dad had given him was never found, and he still reaches for them now, even though it was 12 years ago.

The van itself proved elusive; it kept cropping up on CCTV, playing peekaboo between Brighton and Eastbourne, but the cops couldn't catch it. About a fortnight later, it was used in a robbery at an off-licence in Eastbourne, so it had probably been nicked to fill with stolen drink, and the tools were seen as taking up valuable booze space. Having stolen a load of liquor, the thieves dumped the van, but before they abandoned it they smashed it up. Cheers, lads.

Adam got a phone call from the cops one morning saying, 'Oh, your van's been recovered. It's in the police pound over in Eastbourne.'

When they described the sorry state of it, he said, 'Well I don't really want it then.'

They said, 'Never mind that. You have to collect it.'

In the middle of a job, he asked if it was alright to leave it a few days. He needed to finish his work quickly and get paid, having already lost time finding and buying another vehicle.

'No,' they said; it was going to cost him hundreds of pounds a day. This seemed a bit rich – he'd just been a victim of crime through no fault of his own. Despite explaining he couldn't even get to it from where he was straight away didn't stop him from having to spend more than the van's value in fees.

It was pretty knackered, so he got some new lights for it, tidied it up and sold it on to another fan of jalopies, having already bought a Volvo estate to replace it and to get them through the next stage. This was another, marginally less dilapidated, old heap he drove into the ground. He'd had a really nice vehicle for the first time the year before, but since selling it to buy the bus, it was back to the old game of buying tired old rubbish for peanuts.

Recyclonomics

Half-way through the conversion, Adam ran out of money again, so he had to pause and do some paid work. He would do carpentry for a month or two – cupboards, shelves and kitchens in a house mostly, but sometimes something more interesting or ambitious like Simon's guitar shop in Hammersmith, the Apple Store in Hove, some curvy changing rooms in a shop in The Lanes, or a bar in Kemptown – then he'd come back to the stableyard and carry on. It took about eight months' work to convert the bus, spread over the course of a year. He worked on it at weekends when he could, so it was seven days' work each week one way or another, all the way through the project.

Devon was an absolute diamond about the whole build. She'd just get on with her homework upstairs while Adam finished off downstairs – he'd work till he couldn't do any more, then they'd head back home for supper, bath and bed. Keeping them going financially through this period was no joke, but Devon really pulled her weight with morale, full of enthusiasm for whatever he'd just built.

The lower deck of the bus, viewed from the rear

Adam with his solar panels

For budgetary and ecological reasons, Adam was determined to use as much recycled and second-hand material as possible. As the idea developed and the project took shape as a recycling project, it seemed more and more metaphorically green. He particularly enjoyed Wombling and upcycling materials, and selling off excess parts so that other people could do the same. One man's trash is another man's treasure, after all.

There's a keen market for bus parts, especially seats. He sold them in pairs: one left with one right, thinking they'd make good seating for either side of a breakfast bar or small table. The seats didn't have four legs – the window side was originally secured to the bus wall with screws although the aisle side had legs. People wouldn't pay much – £40 a seat – but he could have sold a thousand of them they were so popular. Even George had two. People loved the classic retro fabrics, the utilitarian shape and chrome details. They travelled from all over the UK in vans to collect them.

Adam became obsessed with looking in skips to see if there was anything he could use or sell. I've read that people have found amazing stuff in skips, like coffins, an Ivor Novello award and a caravan, though I'm not sure I believe that last one. Don't try this at home though if you want to stay on the right side of the law: skip-hunting or dumpster-diving is technically illegal, although I confess it wouldn't stop me. It's rare for anyone to bother prosecuting, since stuff in skips is mostly abandoned, but technically you could be done under the Theft Act of 1968. Petty, I know. You can also be had for trespass if the skip's on private property.

What with all the sockets and switches in the bus, it needed a sizable fuse box. The obvious place for that was under the stairs. When it was used as a bus, that was where the heater was housed, so there was ducting designed to take heat upstairs. Adam repurposed that as a cable housing and used it as an easy way to feed the cables to the top deck.

He wanted to keep and reuse as many of the original bus signs as possible so that it kept its transport identity and character. There were instructions in the bathroom asking people not to talk to the driver, to ensure they had the correct change, and insisting there must be no smoking.

Balance and Bling

Decoration would all come later, so once he'd earned some cash it was at last time to start work downstairs. The weather was warmer by then, allowing him to move his workshop outside and start the detailed planning of the lower deck, starting with the kitchen and living area.

The position of the log burner was already set, since he'd had to make sure it lined up with the wall between the two bedrooms upstairs. From there, he had to work forwards to the staircase. The bus doors were at the front, so if you hopped on and turned towards the back, you had the driver's cab to your left, then the stairway, a gap, the log burner, and quite a bit of space behind that. He decided the only place he could put the shower, boiler and toilet, all in one room, was in that gap just to the rear of the stairs.

That meant he needed the kitchen to be on the other side of the bus, to balance out the heavy weight of the bathroom, boiler and wood burner. The cheapest base units he could find were the starting point for the kitchen. He hoped to jazz them up a bit later by sprinkling some fairy dust. He bought a 400 mm wide drawer unit, a 400 mm cupboard, a 600 mm free-standing gas cooker and a 1200 mm sink unit. Lined up, they filled the space on the right as far as the step up to the back half of the bus. With a second-hand oak worktop and an old Belfast sink and taps found in his garage, the basics were in place. So far, so functional, but it was pretty bland.

To give this kitchen a bit of Big Green Bus bling he bought ready-cut Perspex panels with polished edges online. He chose a couple in every shade of green they had, in the right sizes for the cupboards and drawers, and stuck them to the fronts with contact adhesive: not sophisticated, but effective. Once the handles were on they looked great – quirky and bright. There was a raised luggage rack by the door at the front, so he fitted more kitchen storage above that. He'd found an old wooden cupboard with a compartment for vinyl albums in a skip, so he built that in on top and used it for crockery, reserving the record rack section for bottles of oil and wine.

Next to the kitchen was an area for a small shelf, and opposite that was the log burner. The floor needed to be raised a little to allow for services like pipes and cables, and to create space for insulation. He had just enough oak flooring left over from a previous job to do the whole lower deck. Once he'd fitted that, the bus felt much more homely and comfortable.

He kept the original seating at the back of the bus: a long bench all the way across, over the engine, then two facing double seats fitted over the wheel arches, forming a generous U-shape. The old fabric was charming and would appeal to bus fans, but it was none too clean after supporting the bottoms of thousands of passengers, so he bought new, thicker foam to make more comfortable cushions, then took those to an upholsterer to get them covered.

He'd managed to buy some end-of-line green material online, left over from a local nightclub refit. Its properties were perfect: it was sick-proof, red-wine-proof, fire-proof – ideal for all eventualities, but he worried the colour might be too vivid. He was skint, so it wasn't until his friend Bic lent him some cash that he could go and collect it. When he picked up the fabric his worst fears were confirmed – it was a hellish luminous lime, and he feared he'd really gone overboard with the theme; but, actually, when it was all finished, it looked good. The bright colours may in fact have been part of the reason for the eventual appeal of the bus to families.

He built a six-seater table in between the bench seats. The table was on two legs that slotted into sockets in the floor, similar to the arrangement in some campervans. There was plenty of surface for six people to eat or play games. The table could be removed when you wanted a more open space: he installed a hook that held the tabletop in place as a shutter for the back window. It ended up being one of his favourite features.

Thanks to the sloping floor and site, it was difficult to work out how to make sure the table's sockets and poles ended up at the right length to keep the tabletop level so that his vegetarian scotch eggs wouldn't end up on the floor. The poles tapered, so he couldn't just trim them to size. The only way he could do it was to have one socket level built up. In reference to the roof, he worked out the true level for the table top, then raised one of the sockets, which took a bit of trial and error but he got there in the end. Unfortunately, he forgot to allow for the fact that the bus sits on tyres, and tyre pressure gradually decreases over time. When apples started rolling off the table, he knew it was time to go outside and pump them up again.

To house the log burner safely, he built a plinth and fire-protected area using fireproof materials like Chinese slate and paving slabs for the floor. He cut a hole through to the upper deck and then through the roof for the flue, and, after months of working in the freezing cold, it was of course boiling hot on the day he finally got to test the log burner – which he found worked very efficiently. It continued to do so for years, making the bus usable all year round.

Around this time, he got a bus enthusiast called Dean in over one weekend to help with a few jobs. Just before Dean arrived, Adam was using the angle grinder to finish off some work at the front of the bus, when part of the blade broke off and flew through the air, shattering the window that usually displayed the bus number and destination. Fortunately, Dean sorted that out too, and replaced the original destination with 'Big Green Bus' while he was about it. The windows were still leaking, so they all had to come out, have their seals cleaned, and in some cases replaced, and then be reinstalled using a specialised tool. Dean showed Adam how to remove and replace the panes without smashing them – better late than never.

- 4 -
Reveals on the Bus
From bus to business

[Trigger warning: this chapter mentions suicide. Please reach out if these issues affect you. Text SHOUT to 85258, or call Samaritans on 116 123]

Freshening Up

It was finally time to decorate the interior, which began with filling the many holes he'd drilled, and then sanding down and painting. It was tough to get it done in time, so he was relieved when his dad Brian, a painter and decorator, came and helped. It was a lovely day and his mum Evelyn sat outside on a deckchair, knitting unseasonally and enjoying the sunshine, while Brian helped him indoors. At the start of the project, Brian couldn't see the point of it and thought Adam was wasting his money. Once the TV was involved, he got it, and thought it was a great idea.

At the beginning, Adam had thought of calling his double-decker the Big Blue Bus, since it's alliterative and catchy, but when a friend commented, 'It's probably going to be quite green, isn't it?', meaning ecological and low-impact, he decided that green would fit the whole symbolism of the bus, of small-scale living, better than blue. That decided the colour of the fabric for the seats, the Perspex in the kitchen, and the outside of the bus.

The exterior was a dirty white with orange and red stripes, but Adam wanted the outside to be as attractive as the inside, and literally green. Painting the bus turned out to be a huge task. It all had to be rubbed down with a sander first, and the work had to be done from a hired scaffold tower because it was so high. It took Adam two weeks to finish the blasted thing, using a two-inch brush and a four-inch roller to apply marine paint to resist the elements. Luckily it was summer, but even then it nearly broke him, it was such relentlessly hard work, and of course it needed two coats. His friend Guy the plumber came to help, and Devon did too. The finish was great though, especially where he'd blanked off windows, so it was all worth it.

He thought it would be good to have an outdoor shower as well as the one indoors. Guy the plumber, who'd helped with some of the piping, suggested that in summer this would be refreshing and feel a bit more like a holiday. They found a municipal fixed-head shower unit like the ones in your local swimming pool, with a press-button, timed push switch. It was fed by one pipe, so the water had to go through a regulator first, which they housed under the boiler. That controlled the temperature so that you wouldn't freeze or get scalded. He

Evelyn Woods at the Big Green Bus on painting day

built a screened-off decking area around the showerhead so that he could be in the woodland, listening to the birds and feeling liberated while showering, but without getting muddy feet. It became a surprisingly popular feature.

Running and Falling

By the time Plum were ready to film the reveal, Adam had started to think of the bus less as a surf shack and more as a business and potential main source of income. After many years of having Woods as his trade as well as his surname, full days of carpentry were getting harder, because by now he'd been playing grandmother's footsteps with Ménière's disease for a long time. It's an unpredictable, disconcerting condition: it advances when you least expect it, but you know it's coming sooner or later.

Ménière's causes extreme and unpredictable dizziness and vertigo, with an overwhelming sensation of spinning. Out of nowhere, it can cause a drop attack. Your ears ring and your head spins, as if you're being chucked about in a washing machine on the spin cycle. Before you know what's going on, you vomit, or fall, or both. Some people describe a sensation of being pushed, thrown, shocked or knocked to the ground, or have a sudden illusion of environmental tilt, as if there's been an earthquake. It's a tiny part of the ear that causes all this, this huge effect.

Adam says that during an attack he'd probably choose death if it were offered. If you've ever drunk far too much, then smoked a strong joint and had a whitey, you may have the beginnings of an idea of what it's like. The room spins; your eyes flick from side to side as if you're possessed. With Ménière's, if you're lucky, you don't feel great from the start of the day, so you stay at home and can maybe crawl into bed when necessary. If you're unlucky, you wake up feeling fine, and stay fine until you're in the middle of the supermarket choosing between brands of baked beans. The next thing you know, with no warning at all, a drop attack kicks you in the back of the legs and you find yourself on the floor.

This has consequences for your freedom and quality of life. If you're lucky and fall onto a carpet, you just get a bruise or two. If you're on scaffolding, or cycling, or operating a power tool, it's dangerous and it takes a while to recover. If you were riding a motorbike down a motorway and had an attack, you'd throw yourself off; so if you have attacks with enough regularity you're banned from driving, as with epilepsy. Short attacks might last 20 minutes, but they can go on for up to a day. Most people find them exhausting and need to sleep afterwards.

You know it's bad when the NHS starts offering psychotherapy! It's needed because there's so much anxiety attached to not knowing from one day to the next whether you'll be yourself or a trembling wreck who's letting everyone down and certainly can't drive or use power tools. Anxiety, of course, makes attacks more likely. There's no cure, and when an attack comes, there's no treatment; all you can do is wait it out.

Adam remembers worrying he might have an attack on his wedding day in the nineties, so this has been with him a long time – about 30 years. Imagine this: the venue's decorated, food's made, fizz chilled, all the people you care about have travelled for miles, dressed up and booked hotels, the bride's having her hair done and tickets for the honeymoon are booked... and you're shaking on the floor with ringing in your ears.

This charming combination of nausea, vertigo, vomiting, tinnitus and the resulting falls and injury takes its toll and arrives suddenly, so he feels he has to be on his guard and to take as much preventive action as possible through his diet and fitness. It makes him feel dog-tired some days, and sometimes he can't work at all. When he started having to let people down, his reputation, confidence and self-esteem suffered. Having to take weeks off in the middle of

Regular running with Salbo for company has helped with strength and morale

month-long carpentry jobs in people's homes, when they were relying on him to do what he'd said he'd do, became unfeasible.

To help himself, Adam runs every other day, for miles. Running's silly really, I know. Why bother if there's no one chasing you? They say it prolongs your life by two or three years, but how long do you have to spend running to achieve that? Perhaps it's just wasting time now to buy more time later. If someone told me I was about to die but I could have an extra three years if I preferred, I'd say yes, but if they said, 'You've got to spend that whole time running,' I might not be so keen. Might just take the hit.

But seriously, running has been a big deal for Adam, with Salbo keeping him company, and he thinks it's saved his life. He's tried to keep his body strong: having been a carpenter and a drummer wasn't a bad starting point, and he thinks that's contributed to his current feeling that he's coming to terms with the disease and beating it psychologically. He's tried to protect his immune system through diet too, in this internal war he's fighting. The alternative is giving up.

People from Jessie J and Huey Lewis to Les Paul and Emily Dickinson have struggled with Ménière's; some people have committed suicide as a result, and many more report coming close, including Adam in the past, but he now feels he can win. Having seen his friend Tim Smith, much-loved leader of the influential genre-bending band Cardiacs, keep going for so long with very little movement and no speech due to dystonia (with the committed support of his family and friends) puts things in perspective. Adam's friend Paul, dealing with paralysis from a surfing injury, is also an inspiration. In the sense that he can run, see and smell, is alive, can get up, go out and do things, Adam feels lucky and his drive to leap in, make life up as he goes along, play it by ear is as strong as ever.

Deafness and Drumming

Ménière's is not only chronic but progressive, so you gradually become deaf, which has a whole raft of other side-effects. Adam's plan A was to work as a musician, a drummer. In the nineties he was in the band Zu, with a proper record deal with Chrysalis and a worldwide tour lined up, supporting Hole. He enjoyed living as a professional, waged musician for three years or so – but drumming had to go when his hearing deteriorated.

He's always loved listening to other people's music too, and going to gigs, festivals and clubs, but that's all in the past now too as he can't enjoy it. It leaves a big gap. It's got to the point where he can't listen to new music at all – he can't pick out the melody, even with his amazing hearing aids in, so he experiences it as a mess, as unbearable noise. I didn't realise before that this is a common problem for the deaf, as their perception of both pitch and rhythm can be distorted, and they can experience tinnitus, hyperacusis (extreme sound sensitivity) or diplacusis (experiencing different pitches or timings in each ear). Hearing aids are generally designed to prioritise understanding of speech, and can make music sound even worse than it does without them.

Pubs and anywhere else with background noise are difficult, as he can't separate out the conversation from other sounds, such as rustling crisp packets and clinking glasses. It can make things lonely, as it becomes harder to socialise. He can see people one to one but any more than that is pretty exhausting, which creates a danger of social isolation. All in all, the effects of hearing impairment take a long time to get used to, and limit potential workplaces too.

Everyone's hearing loss is different. In Adam's case he's lost bass, leaving everything sounding tinny and shrieky. If you listen to music you know really well, your memory fills in the gaps with incredible cunning. He sometimes has periods of remission – of suddenly being able to hear a little better, which is tantalising. The last attack he had was so bad that, at first, he couldn't walk

(top) Zu: Melanie Garside, Adam Woods and Paul Godfrey. (bottom) Adam playing drums for Zu

without a stick. On the other hand, his hearing came back to such an extent that he didn't need his hearing aids for a while. Music sounded so beautiful it brought him to tears. When these rare moments of respite occur, he just spends hours listening to his favourite music on headphones.

He doesn't know how much of his improved balance is caused by his brain adapting to his condition, and how much is due to running, but the walking stick isn't necessary any more. He's still a little too dizzy to be able to ride a motorbike or push bike safely, and he can't surf any more either, which is a loss. It's just as well he thought of something else to do with the bus in the end. Tightrope-walking across the Grand Canyon is right out!

Ménière's usually starts in your forties and occurs most often in women. Adam started having Ménière's very young though, when he was only about 21. It started in his left ear, and went through a series of developments including drop attacks, before fading out, leaving behind its damage: tinnitus, deafness and dizziness. If you're really unlucky, it then starts from scratch in your second

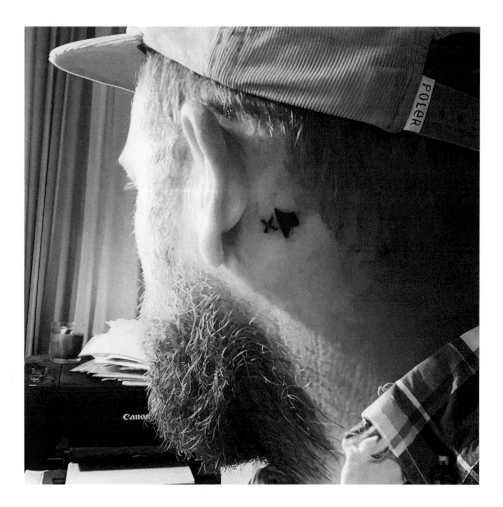

ear, which is what happened to Adam when he was about 40. This was a bitter pill to swallow, and means his hearing loss is bilateral, which is only the case in about 15% of sufferers. On a positive note though, it's gradually burning itself out. You don't get your hearing back, and you may have impaired balance, but after a while you don't have attacks.

He was talking to a musician friend – Bob of Levitation and the Milk and Honey Band – about missing the creative side of his life, especially drumming, and Bob suggested channelling his artistic, expressive energies into visual art instead. He told Bob he was crap at all that and preferred to make things that were useful, but later went away and thought about it, and decided to give it a try. His friend Julian's mum, Amy, is a great potter, and a few years back she had kindly let him have a go with her wheel to try it out. Remembering how much he'd enjoyed that, he signed up for a pottery course in Brighton.

It was a big challenge for him, this. Not only had education been a nightmare the first time around, it felt really challenging going somewhere new where he didn't know anyone, while becoming increasingly deaf but not yet comfortable admitting that to strangers. It felt embarrassing, not being able to hear, and he was still denying it, mourning it. That never really ends. Adam still dreams he can hear, then wakes up to complete silence. Without his hearing aids at night, the silence inside his head feels very lonely. He's still coming to terms with the fact that it's never coming back.

He's glad he went for the pottery though because the whole experience was great, and after making a few bowls and other things on the course, he jumped in with his usual passion. Having bought a kiln and a wheel, he set himself up in a shed by the entrance to the bus site to make mugs and plates. His natural designs, like the imprint of a fern leaf, are inspired by the woodland around him. He sells them to people every now and then (George Clarke has some), and once made a series of bus-branded mugs. It's not the buzz he used to get from playing live to an audience of thousands from a stage in Finsbury Park, but it is satisfying.

He's becoming more comfortable with telling people he's deaf now, and it's less inhibiting that way. He can't talk on the phone easily, which is more of a hindrance than you'd think, but with the help of lipreading and hearing aids, he can facetime.

Nevertheless, as far as income and career were concerned, plan A, music, was already out thanks to deafness. Plan B, carpentry, was on its way out too thanks to other features of Ménière's. Plan C was the bus, which would allow him time to develop his creativity in other ways alongside it, with pottery for example. There's a fair bit of creativity involved in doing conversions as well. Adam's become increasingly confident with making creative as well as practical decisions about colour, materials, design and accessories as he's gone along, thanks to the positive feedback he's received.

Adam throwing a pot on the wheel, and one of his finished pieces

Glamping

Adam manages his Ménière's, like about 120,000 other people in the UK, and many more dealing with worse things, but from a practical point of view it was getting to the stage where he needed to find sustainable work that was really flexible. He needed to not push himself too much and, ideally, do something he really enjoyed. Perhaps it was also becoming clear that he wouldn't be able to surf for much longer, so wouldn't get much use from a surf shack.

As the bus inched closer to completion, he realised that this flexibility might be possible if he hired it out, especially with the TV publicity. It might be a cool thing to run it as a business and rent it out for glamping, a portmanteau term for glamorous camping to let people who can't or don't want to rough it get close to nature. Back in 2013, glamping wasn't a commonly used word. If you wrote it down, people would just assume that you'd spelt camping wrong. Luxury camping wasn't as common as it is now, so he thought perhaps there was a gap in the market for a bus, and he could get involved with that.

Glamping is an ancient idea though. Luxury camping goes back to at least the 16th century for Ottoman and European royalty, with a lot of fancy pennants and luxuries. It developed further through safaris in African tourism of the 19th century, giving access to both creatures and creature comforts. The movement has been building for a while in the UK, thanks to groups like the Landmark Trust, which restores ruined historic buildings, then rents them out, and initiatives like Feather Down Farms, which has been helping farmers to earn a supplementary income from glamping for two decades. Glamping started to take off in the UK in about 2010, but wasn't well known till later, entering the *Oxford English Dictionary* in 2016, when the bus had been going for a couple of years. Since then, problems with the cost of living, films like *Nomadland* and TV programmes like *George Clarke's Amazing Spaces* have broadened awareness of small spaces.

Most people have many possessions around them – sentimental things you wouldn't logically keep but you don't want to throw away. Adam's got stuff in storage himself – pictures, old report cards from school. It enhances a sense of lightness on holiday to be free of all that excess baggage. It's a nice change to be somewhere small, where there's a place for everything and everything's in its place. There's nothing unnecessary cluttering up the surfaces. The ingenuity of the storage and space solutions, like in a boat or caravan, can be satisfying.

With the cost-of-living challenges we all have now, it's cheaper to heat and to power small spaces, and it just feels more manageable all round. So now there's a big community of van dwellers, many of whom have jobs and live full, otherwise recognisably normal lives, rather than necessarily being part of a subculture as they would have been a couple of decades ago.

A whole genre of non-fiction and a category of holiday rentals has evolved to do with off-grid and eco-glamping, digital detox, van life, mobile living,

downsizing, cabins, campers and conversions, retreats and unusual dwellings. Websites like Canopy & Stars, Coolstays and Host Unusual give access to these, following in the footsteps of the Landmark Trust, which has been renting out towers, follies and lighthouses for decades. The industry is worth billions in the UK, which is a world leader in this area, and the exponential growth of the past decade is predicted to continue.

There's a green motivation as well: many people now shun short-haul flights for ecological reasons, and stay inland, leading to more portmanteau terms like staycation and holistay. Perhaps the growth of Center Parcs has helped too, by making it normal for family holidays to be fun and outdoorsy, without being under canvas. Now you can sleep in anything from bell tents and geodesic domes, yurts, tipis, pods, cabins and safari tents to vintage caravans, shepherd's huts and tree houses. These are often low-impact and small-scale compared with big hotels you might fly to in an aeroplane, and you're literally closer to nature too. It tends to be quieter staying somewhere small, so you're more likely to see and hear wildlife.

Now that Adam was thinking of the bus as a business, he needed a logo. He wanted something simple and clear that emphasised the natural setting, the literal and metaphorical greenness of the place and the familiarity of the double-decker bus shape – that tapered, risen-loaf silhouette. The half-profile design looks like catching sight of the bus with its lights on, in front of pine trees, after walking up a hill. It was his idea, but the final version was put together by a friend of an ex-girlfriend, called Roberto Hansel. Adam was so pleased with it that he had it printed onto enamel plates and cups, to help brand the bus and make it memorable.

Seaside Launch

As the big reveal approached, Plum Pictures found and rented space at a nearby glamping site for the day of the shoot. It was an attractive place, in a field near Ditchling. However, the bus wasn't insured because it was on SORN, a statutory off-road notification that meant Adam couldn't drive it there. He told Plum they'd have to pay the tax and insurance if they wanted the bus driven to another location, as he couldn't afford it. On top of that, the bus was too high to get past the trees at the entrance to their chosen site, so they even hired a tree surgeon to cut back branches before its arrival.

Adam drove the bus there in the morning, managed to get it into the appointed field, washed it, and got it all ready. It was a lovely summer's day – the perfect day for 'after' shots. An amazing stylist and author, Jane Field-Lewis, the brains behind *Amazing Spaces*, came along to dress the build to show it at its best. She even brought hired props to pep it up a bit. It looked a million dollars – not just the million hours it felt like it had taken. Adam tried to make a mental note of everything the professionals did, so he could replicate it later, once midnight had struck and the bus turned back into a pumpkin.

He'd made the main area his priority, leaving the shower room until last, suspecting he wouldn't have the time or money to be able to finish everything. This meant anything unfinished could be behind a shut door for the purposes of the 'reveal' programme, so he needed a door to hide the work in progress that was the shower room. The skip-hunted solution he ended up with was a lovely old ledged and braced door from a 1940s outhouse. Once he'd sanded it down, the layers of paint looked quite psychedelic, so he kept the door like that rather than painting it.

The bus was filmed for the big reveal without the bathroom done, but it was fine, because it became clear that Plum Pictures love that sort of thing, saying, 'Ooh! You said what you were going to do and you couldn't finish it!' That humanised the project and made for good telly from their point of view. They found a toilet from somewhere and propped it in position to give an impression of the finished layout, and there was no time to plumb in the outdoor shower, so they strapped it to a hose as a quick fix to show the effect – a little smoke and mirrors and TV magic. But Adam got it all finished soon afterwards, so when they called him back for the Christmas Special, it was all done.

Then George arrived. He likes to avoid seeing any finished conversion in advance, wanting the surprise of it being so good (or not) that his reaction shows all over his face for real, for the cameras. Adam was nervous, waiting for him to come in and be filmed walking around the bus, really wanting him to like it after all that time. It would have felt awful if he'd been underwhelmed, but it was fine because George seemed blown away. He thought it was ingenious, the way Adam had fitted the bunks in the back upstairs, really dug the sliding

Adam using the outdoor shower

doors that disappeared into the panelled wall, loved the collage wallpaper Devon had made around the staircase, and was just really into the hand-made feel of the whole place.

Of course, there's a bit of artful construction in TV programmes, but Adam was pleasantly surprised by how authentic the experience ended up feeling. At heart, the show is about George guiding viewers through the ups and downs of the process, but he's genuinely enthusiastic, connecting with makers and appreciating their kooky little builds on their own terms.

After the reveal had been filmed, but before series 2 of the show had even aired, Plum Pictures called to ask Adam to be on the Christmas Special as well, but that was before he'd found the bus a home, so he drove it off the yard and parked it up on Brighton seafront to give it a prettier setting. Plum filmed the special there in October, eating unseasonal mince pies and so on. They also chose his project as one of the few they included in the book they released about the series in 2014.

Everyone with projects included in the Special also had to go to a 'Christmas market' Plum had mocked up, to be interviewed. Adam sat in the green room with the others, waiting ages for his turn to be interviewed, grumbling. What hard work it was having TV involved; how no one would put themselves through it without a business to promote; how it was only the publicity for the bus rental business that made it worth it; and so on. He was embarrassed to discover that, other than Barry with his 'Hivehaus', the others had all converted places for themselves, not as businesses, and were happy just to be on TV. Oops.

Devon, Adam and George at the Big Green Bus

Adam drove the bus down to the seafront again around Christmas to hold open days to promote his glamping offering. He parked up where the coaches drop their Women's Institute ladies off for a day out. The parking warden came and ticked him off, saying, 'You can't park there!'

Adam feigned confusion. 'Why not? I'm a bus!'

The warden eyed him wearily, decided a row would be too much like hard work and trudged off, shaking his head.

Devon and he had their open day on the Saturday, making mulled wine, lighting the fire, giving out mince pies and handing out leaflets. Passers-by popped in for a nose around to see if it really was 'As seen on TV'. Then Adam and Devon shut the doors, cooked some dinner and enjoyed living on the seafront for a weekend. Not the surfing holidays they'd planned, but still by the sea, and still brilliant. They'd do another open day on Sunday, then drive the bus back to the countryside.

- 5 -
All Aboard

Finding a home and running a rental

Moorhens and Marriages

After shooting the reveal, Adam needed to think about leaving the yard and finding a place for the bus to go. Having decided to turn the bus into a business, he needed an address so that he could get a website up and running and market it, ready for when the TV show was aired. He didn't want to miss the chance to take advantage of the publicity of millions of people watching it – a few of them might want to come and stay on the bus. If short-lived, spontaneous curiosity led them to look for the Big Green Bus on the internet, there needed to be a site for them to find.

He put a tweet out and managed to find a place near Lewes. Someone asked, 'Have you tried this couple? They do weddings and things.' When he went along to meet them, it turned out they were married couple Gilly and Jed, whom he knew already from when he'd first moved to Brighton. They were both journalists: she used to write a yearly guide – *The Juicy Guide to Brighton & Hove* – and is now an award-winning food writer and podcaster; he's a journalist and senior lecturer in journalism at the University of Brighton. They'd moved out to quite a big place in the sticks and used to host weddings on the site, especially in the summer. Quite big they were – micro-Glastonbury type affairs, with cocktail bars, bands playing – a lovely vibe.

Adam headed to Lewes and walked around the site with Jed, Gilly and their neighbour, Demolition Dave. Salbo, his faithful, well-behaved companion went too. The plan was that Dave would head back over with his digger once they'd chosen a location, and level the land off for ready for the concrete base Adam would need to lay for the bus. They found a lovely spot, next to a pond with moorhens, Jed's pride and joy. They were all chatting and walking around the pond to pick the right spot when Adam heard a sudden intake of breath and turned to see Jed staring at Salbo, who was looking balefully at them with her mouth full of slack moorhen. Not very diplomatic – he'd only had her a short while and already she was bringing shame on the family. He managed to get her to drop the bird but it clearly had a broken wing and everyone assumed it was a goner.

Jed was shaking his head as Adam apologised profusely. Volunteering to put it out of its misery, Adam said 'Don't worry!' I'll take care of this,' trying to put a practical face on things. In reality, he was miserable, having never killed an animal in his life; apart from anything else he's a vegetarian. Having seen people pull chickens' necks, making it look easy, he told himself it would be alright but, wanting to stun the poor thing first at least, he walked off to do that by a tree.

Unfortunately, he was rubbish at it. Hitting its head weakly against the trunk, the bird just looked at him as if to say, 'What the hell do you think you're doing?' Adam didn't have another plan, so he hit it again but it still didn't work so, in a panic, he started whacking it against the tree as hard as he could until its head fell off. Hideous. Turning around slowly, breathing heavily, he saw the others staring at him as though he was a psychopath. Auspicious beginning.

Demolition Dave came and levelled the land, and Adam put down a concrete base with the help of Nick, his brother-in-law. Before the bus could be brought on site, the decking area needed to be built, and drainage and power installed. It took a lot of work and materials, and when it was time to drive the bus to the site, it got horribly stuck and had to be dragged into position using Dave's digger. After that, everyone sat back and waited for the show to air.

Airtime and Teething Problems

Between two and three million people watched the show (*George Clarke's Amazing Spaces*, series 2, episode 3: 'Double-decker Retreat and Boat Hotel') live on Channel 4 on 7 November 2013, as the series was so popular. Many more saw it later, as of course there are loads of reruns and you can watch it online even now. The episode was popular even compared with the series as a whole: only three of its 97 shows have a higher audience rating according to episoderatings.com.

The bus was sold out for months by the end of the show's first airing – an even better result than Adam had hoped for. From there, it became very popular, without needing much special effort from Adam. He'd done his best to design something practical and charming where people could enjoy themselves, but there was more to it than that. Having been on telly helped – gave it a bit of glamour perhaps.

Once something's been on TV, other production companies start asking to film it too, so the bus has been on screen a lot. Also on Channel 4, *George Clarke's Amazing Christmas Spaces* aired on 19 December 2013, which fuelled interest and bookings further. The bus was later filmed for a second Channel 4 show called *Four in a Bed* – a reality hotel competition show in which 'B&B owners throw open their doors and take turns to stay with each other, as they compete to be crowned best hosts'. This show is even more popular, with over a thousand episodes. The bus featured in series 11, episode 33, aired on 9 November 2016.

After the experience with Plum Pictures, Adam was always up for a bit of free marketing, so he was keen for the bus to be featured on *Four in a Bed*.

He'd been going out with a woman called Susan for a week or so when he applied, so he asked her if she'd like to be involved. He thought they'd have to exaggerate the length of their relationship, assuming that the producer only wanted established couples where both partners were involved in the B&B business. This turned out to be nonsense: he could have just gone on his own, but it added a little conspiratorial spice during filming, by which time they'd been together a month or two.

The series works in mini-cycles of five programmes, filmed over a fortnight, involving the hosts of four B&B businesses. It begins with a dinner at the first venue, giving all the hosts a chance to meet one another. The idea is that they have a relaxed discussion about being a B&B host and reveal enough about their character to build interest for the viewer, as well as expectations about the hosts' properties and their likely conflicts and attitudes to one another's hosting.

The trouble is that it goes on for absolutely hours, this meal, so that enough filming can be done as the director gives the hosts conversation prompts to see what works. Hosts aren't allowed to do more than pick at the food, because the plates need to look similar throughout the meal for continuity reasons. The same goes for the wine, which is free and plentiful, presumably in the hope of livening up the chat a little – it too has to look the same throughout the meal, so the moment you take a sip, it's someone's job to top it up. It's treacherously easy to lose track of how much you've drunk.

So, at this dinner in Weymouth, the first host told the others her B&B had been featured in *Tatler* and in *Vogue*. It felt a little surprising, given the conventional appearance of the place, but the conversation moved on. After the meal, the group was split up and the hosts were interviewed on camera either in pairs or alone. Too drunk to be wary, Susan repeatedly expressed her surprise about *Tatler* and *Vogue* before Adam could warn her, though he was squeezing her hand as hard as he could. When he mentioned to her afterwards that she might have come on a bit strong, she got very upset, and wanted to back out altogether and go home, worrying she'd gone too far.

They agreed to discuss it in the morning, but by then Susan felt even more distressed. They called the producer, who came over early for emergency talks. When they explained the problem, he told them everyone had said the same sort of thing, so while he couldn't guarantee they wouldn't use the clip, they'd edit it if they did and it wouldn't be embarrassing. Susan managed to keep going, but the whole thing became a bit of a strain. She wasn't speaking to Adam by the final episode, where the hosts and viewers find out how much the other hosts have underpaid or overpaid for each stay.

Months later, when the show aired, Adam invited Susan round to the flat to watch it for a laugh with him and Devon, over a bottle of wine and a takeaway. Just before it started Susan said, 'Oh, I hope they don't use that clip of me on the first night.' Well, the show started, and they had indeed used it, the cads – the whole thing. She wouldn't stay for the rest, just got up and left. It turned out to be even worse than that: they'd actually used the clip as part of the recap at the start of every episode of the mini-series, so it was impossible to miss it.

Adam had some surprising requests after that, like a call from ITV asking him if a stay on the bus could be a prize on *Catchphrase*! Perhaps the most startling was a request to shoot an adult film on the bus, which he declined. The second time someone asked the same thing they even offered him a starring role as a sweetener! Momentarily tempted, it was still a no – he didn't think it would do much for his family-friendly marketing strategy.

The bus was always popping up in print media too, from magazines to national newspapers. It even became famous in the USA after appearing on an episode of *Extreme RVs* (series 5, episode 7: 'Racer's Paradise', 11 September 2019). RVs are 'recreational vehicles', the American term for motorhomes, caravans and campers. The crew came all the way over from the States to film that, so they must have had some crazy budget, or perhaps just fancied a holiday.

The bus was also on a couple of Dutch programmes, a French one, and a Belgian one on 27 October 2018 called *Une Brique dans le Ventre*. The show's name translates as 'a brick in the belly', an idiomatic expression meaning that all Belgians are born wanting to build their own house, to express individuality through their home. Belgians were interested partly because, 'Le bus à 2 étages est un véritable symbole anglais'. In the show, Adam's voice was dubbed, so he had the bonus pleasure of watching himself sounding as though he spoke fluent French.

With people even coming from abroad to visit the bus, the venture was set up for success. People were becoming fascinated by small living at the time, and the bus rode that wave. It wouldn't have the same impact now – fewer people watch things live on terrestrial TV, and the market for reality shows about design, makeovers and interiors is pretty saturated, but back then it made all the difference. Adam was recognised in ASDA, for goodness' sake! A taste of fame!

Once the bus was settled on its permanent site, all pre-booked, Adam opened the doors to paying guests for the first time. From the start, most guests were complimentary and appreciative, and many became repeat customers. He's always tried to keep standards high, although everyone makes mistakes, but anyone who runs a similar business will tell you that a small minority of customers do seem to get a kick out of finding fault or feel the urge to offer unsolicited advice about how to do things differently. Adam soon found that a complimentary bottle of fizz and some brownies took the focus off unimportant minor details for all but the most negative-minded guests. You can't please everyone, but most guests really were more than fair and left great reviews.

The site had a few teething problems though. The weddings Jed and Gilly were running on the site were lovely, but the bus was right next to the field where they were held, so Adam couldn't rent the bus out when those events were on, which was a problem. They came to an agreement where the bride and groom would use the bus as their bridal suite, which usually worked well. Sometimes, however, it didn't. At one of the weddings, the guests shoved all the kids in the bus to keep them out of the way, so when Adam went the next day it was trashed – full of mud and breakages.

Towards the end of that first summer, disaster struck when Gilly and Jed received a Stop Notice from the local council. It turned out that some local people were upset by the extra cars and noise, and discovered that planning consent should have been sought for the wedding business and hadn't been. Jed and Gilly hadn't realised they needed it, so they didn't have permission for a double-decker bus on the land either. The bus and Adam himself were seen locally as being part of the same problem, although he had no idea he'd been doing anything wrong.

A group of local people got so angry about it all that they did some unpleasant things, including direct vigilante action like deliberately firing their shotguns and revving quad bikes during wedding vows. This wasn't quite the vibe the couples had been hoping for from their bucolic nuptials, and it didn't go down well. On another occasion, one of the neighbours arranged wheelie bins all across the lane to make it awkward for guests to leave, which caused an accident. Lovely.

Inevitably, the council shut them down. By pleading, Adam managed to negotiate with them to let him finish the summer season, but that was it. There was no point in him trying to get planning permission to keep the bus on someone else's land, so the search for a home for the bus began again. It had already become clear that the experiment had worked: the bus was a functional, manageable venture. It was hard work to manage the changeovers and maintain everything, but having this business lessened the pressure of the Ménière's. He needed to find a place the bus could stay for good.

The Great Glamping Gamble

Demolition Dave, who owned the farm next door, said, 'I've got a bit of land I might sell,' so Adam went to have a look. It was very rough on the surface, full of scrap bits of car and tractor, but with a bit of work he could see it would be perfect. It was a little piece of secluded woodland near Whitesmith, and crucially it had road access. This was important because it's very hard to get permission for new road access onto lanes. Adam had already found out how hard it was to track down suitable locations for the bus, so he was delighted.

However, Dave didn't really need to sell the land and started to go off the idea. Adam offered him £40,000, way over market value, because he needed to

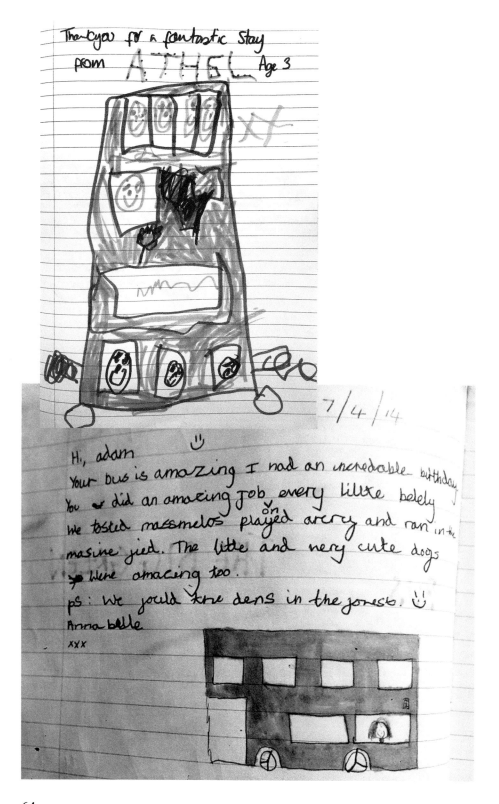

Thankyou for a fantastic stay from A T H E L Age 3

7/4/14

Hi, adam

Your bus is amazing I had an incredable birthday. You did an amaeing job every lillte belely We tosted massmelos played arcry and ran in the masine jied. The little and nery cute dogs where amacing too.

ps: We jould tire dens in the jorest.

Annabelle

xxx

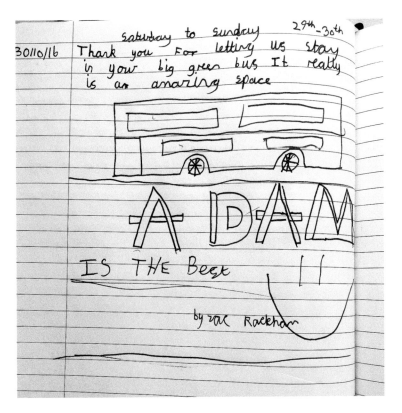

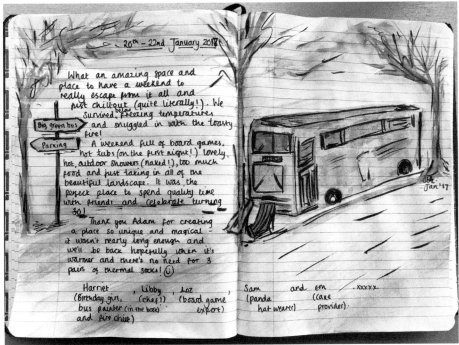

Notes from lovely Big Green Bus guests

do the deal quickly. The bus was mothballed, earning nothing until a home was found for it, so he was glad when Dave finally accepted. Adam was gambling, because the land was worth much less, and was agricultural, and the Stop Notice had made it clear that planning permission would be needed, which he did not yet have. He just had to cross his fingers and hope it would be granted.

Having his offer for the site accepted was all very well, except that Adam didn't have any money. The bank wasn't keen to step in. He'd ploughed all the summer's profits back into the original site, not dreaming it would last such a short time. It had cost thousands, all that concrete and decking, so there were lessons to be learnt. He'd been paying a percentage to rent too, of course. If someone could be persuaded to lend money to a moorhen-murdering bankrupt, he could pay them back gradually by giving them a percentage of the takings and it would be cheaper than the rent at Gilly and Jed's.

Adam's parents couldn't help him out, but our friend David once said he was interested in investing if Adam ever needed him to, bless him. You'd think a financial advisor would know better. Anyway, when Adam got in touch, David was still into it and lent him £60,000 for the land, some legal fees, a base, fencing and so on. What a gent. The deal was that Adam would pay interest (because David's not a complete fool) and finish paying the loan back after three years or David would get a portion of the business. Adam's far too much of a lone wolf to share, so there was good motivation to make it work.

So far, it was going well. Land? Check. Money? Check. Next stop, planning, which is where he really came unstuck. The application went in promptly but there was a massive problem. He'd underestimated the knock-on effects of local feeling about the wedding business. Locals formed an action group against the bus – imaginatively called 'No Big Green Bus', with a logo like a road sign, badges – the lot. They were committed, and they had a badge-making machine.

Very anxious about the financial effects of potential delays, Adam started to clear the site, but he couldn't create a base or move the bus for the time being. So many objections were made to his plans that he had to submit them to a Planning Committee, which is like a courtroom with eight councillors. You get to say your bit, those objecting get to do the same, and the councillors make a decision. There's only one committee meeting per month and they get very booked up, so Adam had to wait a couple of months, coughing up to employ a planning consultant and then sitting on his hands and sweating money.

In the meantime, there was a parish council meeting. Adam went along with his planning consultant to see if he could defuse the situation. It was one of the most frightening things he'd ever done in his life. The locals who were objecting were very angry – so much so that some were shouting and others were crying. It was bewildering to Adam, since all he wanted to do was put a bus in a wood he owned and host one family at a time, cooking marshmallows and spotting fungi.

He had five minutes, officially, to try to explain that this wasn't a party bus for stags and hens, that he was not the criminal mastermind behind the weddings, and so on. His five minutes were interrupted over and over by furious locals though, so the Chair kept having to call the meeting to order. In the end it took about 35 minutes for him to have his five-minute say. No one seemed to trust him or want to listen to him and the whole thing felt most unpromising. He dreaded the Planning Committee meeting even more after that.

While waiting, Adam had to employ a biodiversity consultant, and pay for investigations to be done on the land, looking for particular newts and so on that might be adversely affected by any development. He spent £15,000 on all that. The whole endeavour was probably the biggest gamble of his life. Insanity, really. Anyone sensible would likely have given up at this point, if they had even got there. If Adam didn't get planning consent, he'd have to sell the bus to repay even half of what he owed, leaving him tens of thousands in debt, and all his work would have been for nothing.

Having waded in this far, he couldn't afford to lose – a position he seems to find himself in quite a lot – no reverse gear, remember? We do not retreat. Forward, to adventure! So, in preparation for the Planning Committee meeting, he canvassed the local councillors as much as was allowed, explaining what he was trying to do: run a one-off, eco-friendly holiday home for families, bring revenue to the area, encourage guests to support the local pub and shop. It was all true, and they needed to know that the bus wasn't going to create a nuisance with lots of traffic, noise and environmental damage.

Before the committee meeting, he was very nervous. The room was absolutely packed – there were hundreds of people – so many that they couldn't all fit in, so the whole event was live-streamed online as well, would you believe? First ASDA, now this. Fame at last. Anyway, he said his piece, as did his expert, and the other side had their say, with their expert.

By the time it got to the vote, Adam felt pretty depressed. The first councillor voted against him, as did the next and his heart sank further. How was he going to dig himself out of this one? The third was in favour, the fourth against, and he could almost taste the other side's excitement. However, at this point the tide turned and the last four councillors sided with Adam. It was 5:3 to the Big Green Bus!

His planning consultant had been in the business 40 years, but even he was so shocked he could barely speak. "Well! I didn't think that was going to happen!" he said. Adam was pretty outraged; the consultant had never mentioned thinking it was a lost cause while Adam paid his fees. The local people were so furious about the result that, when Adam approached the leader to shake his hand after the judgement, he left him hanging and turned away. Very mature.

At last, Adam could move the bus to the site and get on with business. His friend Mike had helped him to get the land ready, and now gave him a hand

The Big Green Bus in its final woodland home

moving the bus to its forever home. It still wasn't plain sailing though, as the locals' bad feeling festered. The original sign mounted on his gate for the Big Green Bus was mysteriously scratched out with a piece of glass. Whenever he greeted his neighbours while walking his dog in the lane they shared, they'd ignore him.

His only hope was to confront them with relentless friendliness and hope that he could wear them down in the end. He now feels that, as someone who's lived mostly in a city, he didn't give enough consideration to the fact that in the country people really don't like too much change in one go. A decade on, some of the old action group have died and others have moved away. Those remaining have softened. He's never had a complaint, about noise or anything, and after ten years of keeping his nose clean he finally feels like a member of the local community, with friendly neighbours.

Luckily, once Adam had got the bus set up in its new home, the bank decided he wasn't such a liability after all and agreed to give him a mortgage on the land, which meant he could pay David off, so everyone was happy. Hilariously, a Planning Committee member who'd been one of most vocal opponents of the bus was fined over £75,000 in 2017 for making changes to her own Grade II listed house without permission, but still did not resign and was made to give up her post. The hypocrisy was staggering, but Adam confesses a better person probably wouldn't have felt the gleeful schadenfreude he did.

Hampers and Campers

Financially, the bus worked well once it was all set up in its forever home. There were no promotion or advertising costs as it sold well though reputation and return custom every year. That meant Adam could concentrate on doing the changeovers – the laundry, repairs, cleaning and so on. He did it mostly himself as the development of his Ménière's meant he definitely couldn't have managed a proper nine-to-five job at this point, or work on the tools. Devon helped with bed-making, for pocket money. As he'd hoped, he'd created an environment in which he could earn enough without excessive work, and all was well.

When the Ménière's got a little worse, he hired in someone to help with the quick turnaround needed for speedy changeovers – when one group leaves at 10 in theory but 11 in practice, and the next arrives at 3. The bus was hardly ever empty in peak season – it was back-to-back bookings. Two local women who ran a company called House Proud Cleaning helped while the bus was at Gilly and Jed's. Later, a woman called Sarah Darling, who lives nearby, helped him to make the venture work by doing a great job of the laundry and cleaning. There was too much to do otherwise, what with the hot tub and outdoor area as well as beds and cleaning inside.

As anyone who's run a holiday rental knows, there's quite a spectrum of ways in which guests leave a property they've been staying in. At one extreme, you wouldn't know they'd been there – it's immaculate. Most people are in the middle – they leave it fairly tidy, maybe strip the beds, let you know about any breakages, and clean up lightly after themselves, which is fine. At the other – well it makes you wonder what their house is like if they can reduce a rental property to total chaos in two days. There'd even be hideous toilet-related business, mess everywhere. Awful.

A day in the life of a host on changeover day goes like this: Adam would usually turn up at 10:20 in the morning to make a start. If you're too early, it panics people and they leave the place in more of a state. He'd strip the beds and gather everything that needed washing, which later would be hanging all over his flat to dry. He'd get any pre-ordered Campfire Hampers ready – these included the ingredients needed for a Big Green Bus chilli to be cooked over the campfire with baked potatoes, a full English breakfast, fruit juice, coffee, local cider and wine, a cheese board with crackers and a lovely cake: enough food and drink for a stay.

At first he'd go and buy things from farm shops himself to fill the hampers, but later he contracted that work out to Laughton village shop, where Allison would pack the hampers with local foods, which guests were very happy with. He made no money on them – they were just a nice service and it's good to feed revenue back into the local area. He also kept bees in hives near the entrance to the woodland, by the solar panels, and their raw honey was available for guests to buy as souvenirs.

Sometimes there'd be wear and tear or repairs to take care of, and since he'd built everything himself, only he knew how to fix things quickly. In the winter, maintenance involved dealing with bursting pipes and so on, as it would get so cold between guests' stays in the low season. It was difficult to go away and leave the business for anyone else to run, which was a little limiting, but the bus was still a massive success overall.

Adam had years of happy guests leaving lovely drawings and messages in the visitors' book. He took particular care to make sure guests were safe, and there were no serious injuries despite years of people using the log burner in place of their usual central heating, lighting the firepit instead of using a microwave, and excited kids racing around an unfamiliar space with lots of trees.

The bus was an especially popular choice for families with children on the autism spectrum – he must have had five or six such families heading down his way every year. Every child's different, but for many kids with autism a change of scene can be difficult or distressing, making family holidays a challenge. Given that, Adam was particularly delighted when these families said the bus holidays were some of their most relaxing ever, for children and parents alike. He doesn't know why it worked so well for them: perhaps their kids had an interest in buses or vehicles, or found them familiar.

Adam tests the hot tub at the Big Green Bus

Guests often commented that they'd particularly enjoyed interacting with nature in the wood. They and their children would look out for animals, mess about with sticks, investigate the treehouse Adam had built near the entrance, cook on an open fire and splash about in the hot tub.

Because there was also a transport business with a similar name, confusion was inevitable. It was called the Big Green Coach, and took people to festivals and gigs, amongst other things. For a decade, Adam got a ridiculous number of enquiries – calls, texts and emails – about getting to see Ed Sheeran on time, fitting their son's bike on the coach, toilet stops on the motorway, finding lost rucksacks and so on. It was frustrating. Sometimes the caller would be so confused, distressed or furious that they wouldn't believe the bus was a rental property when Adam tried to redirect them to the correct website. He consoled himself by posting the redacted, anonymised exchanges for the amusement of his followers.

'I got your number from the internet. Is this service running?'

'Hi. You've called the wrong number. I'm a campsite in Sussex. You need the Big Green Coach company.'

'I have to go to work from Monday by 8 I should be there at my office.'

Adam would reply with the link for the coach company, but to no avail.

'This is my first day. I am nervous since national bus comes here at 8.10.'

'I can't help you,' Adam would text, 'I'm not a bus company. Follow the link above.'

Still, the misguided passenger would persevere: 'The first month I stay in Soham and then I move to Ely better as there is no early start buses here. If you could help me that would be nice Sir.'

'You are texting a campsite!! Click on this link. This is the company that you need to talk to.' He'd insert the link.

'Which link?'

'This link.' He'd insert it again.

'There is no link.'

He'd insert it again twice with a pointy finger underneath.

This sort of thing was a weekly occurrence.

French Leave

Once the bus business was running well, Adam started to cast about for a new project. He'd noticed online that properties in some parts of Europe were very cheap. Thanks to the EU, we had citizenship status conferring freedom of movement of persons, services and goods, so it seemed like a great idea to make the most of that by doing up a place over there for holidays, and possibly rentals or relocation. What could possibly go wrong?

He spotted a house he liked, phoned and spoke to the agent, threw a tent in the van and headed for Newhaven with Devon and the dog. They hopped on a ferry, got off at Dieppe and drove to Limousin to have a look. He'd underestimated how long it would take to get there. Limousin is a volcanic highland region in the north-western part of the Massif Central, so it's all hills, valleys and small mountains, and the roads are narrow, twisting and slow.

The house was very high up, and Adam noticed that his Ménière's symptoms dissipated a little, perhaps from the change in pressure at altitude, he thought. Looking up the height on a map, he wondered whether perhaps, if he could find somewhere that high in the UK, it would be easier for him. Unfortunately, the only place he could find was a hotel in Eryri (Snowdonia) in North Wales, which is a bit far from Sussex. His ear, nose and throat specialist laughed when Adam told him anyway, and suggested it was more likely the lack of pollution and stress that had offered relief.

The drive from Dieppe took about eight hours, and when they got there they met the agent and found that the photos online had misrepresented the house somewhat: it was derelict, with a choked orchard in the back garden obscured by eight-foot-high shrubs worthy of Manderley. The place was 400 years old, with thick walls of blue local granite; the roof was pushing the walls outwards

The French house

and the house was barely standing. Despite it being too dangerous to go inside, it was on the market for 18,000 euros. Adam asked the agent how long it had been up for sale and he said, 'An age'.

'I'm not surprised!' he laughed. 'I wouldn't pay more than 8,000 for it.' This was about £6,000.

'OK,' said the agent, 'I'll put it to the owners,' and hopped in his car, before Adam could explain that it wasn't a formal offer.

Devon and Adam had a lovely day looking around the local area, then drove back to the ferry early the next morning. The agent rang as they got on the ferry to say their offer had been accepted. That's how Adam bought the first house he ever saw in France, though the niceties took a little while.

He bought a van to help him take furniture and materials over there, and every year he'd drive over with Salbo and spend a few weeks sorting it out. A cheap little caravan, bought second hand, gave him something to live in while building. When first towing the caravan over to France he tried a toll-free route on a whim, to explore the country and save some cash. It took far, far longer than expected. Too tired to drive the whole way, he had to pull over to a layby, where he and Salbo slept in the caravan. The hearing aids came out as usual, leaving him almost completely deaf. Allegations have been made about the volume of Adam's snoring. Lies, he says, but deafness can mean you snore until it gets so loud your whole head vibrates before you jolt yourself awake

The caravan where Adam and Salbo stayed while Adam worked on the French house

to find your partner's disappeared, sometimes permanently. Anyway, Salbo doesn't seem to mind it.

The next thing Adam knew, he was awake and Salbo was jumping around, baring her teeth, barking. He sat up just in time to see her launch herself at the caravan door, where he glimpsed a man with a knife, backing away. Adam leapt up in his pants, grabbed a kitchen knife and ran after the man, only to see him jump into a nearby car and drive away. Sleep was impossible after that, so they got back on the road. Since she probably saved his life that night, he forgave Salbo for the moorhen.

Over many visits, Adam strapped the house's walls to stop them spreading, coated them in lime render, cleared the garden of weeds, pruned the trees, laid a lawn, and installed a new septic tank that cost more than the house. Soon the structure was safe and watertight, with new windows. Once he'd worked out that planning applications were handled by the Maire, or local mayor, not a woman called Marie as he originally thought, he even got planning permission to turn it into a three-bedroom house. Despite the reputation of the French for endless bureaucracy, it was pretty plain sailing. In fact, the water and electric were connected for free, which they wouldn't have been in the UK.

Digging a deeper basement in France

As part of these plans, he decided to put a bathroom in the basement. That meant digging two feet of earth from the basement floor to make the ceiling head height, so he hired a digger for a day. This looked like being a laugh: an opportunity to use a vehicle he'd never tried before. The first step was to teach himself how to operate it – he didn't want to knock the house down by mistake, but you know him by now: how hard could it be? To save time, he practised in the basement, getting some of the earth shifted while showing himself the ropes. What could go wrong?

Well, it turns out that it's possible to get your head wedged between a digger and the ceiling of the basement you're digging. With his skull in a headlock of his own devising, he had to think very carefully which lever to press, and in what direction, without being able to turn his head to check. The controls were pretty basic and jerky, so one way would have been certain death, with his cranium crushed like a watermelon. Get it right, and he'd free his head and see another day. He racked his imperilled brains, trying to visualise the controls but, unable to remember, he guessed... and lived to tell the tale.

- 6 -
Fire, Plague, Fire!
The death, resurrection and destruction of the bus

Rolling With the Punches

Then disaster struck.

One morning back in the UK, Adam put his hearing aids in and checked his phone messages, to find that his bus guests had called, saying there was a fire. It's still not clear why it happened, despite the efforts of the fire brigade and insurance company, but there seems to have been a chimney fire. This happens when soot coating the upper part of the flue liner catches fire, and is more likely when burning green or wet fuels.

Chimney fires can be dangerous as they create extremely high temperatures very quickly. Even the wood around the boxing-in of the flue pipe upstairs had caught fire and was charred. The guests fought the fire as best they could, then retreated to call the fire brigade and Adam.

The fire service put out the fire and no one was hurt, but the upstairs of the bus was black and crispy and the whole place absolutely reeked. It was a sorry sight, and Adam's heart sank at the huge amount of work, time and money it was going to take to get his sole source of income up and running again, but at least the damage was only to stuff, not people.

He reported to the insurance company and the next day they sent a loss adjuster. I can't help thinking you've got to have a bit missing to do that job. There you are, on the ravaged site of your broken dreams – your burgled house, your burnt bus, your ruined holiday – while you're beginning to process your feelings and think about how you will deal with the fallout. The loss adjuster turns up and it feels as though all they're doing is trying to catch you out, find ways to tell you it's your own fault. Necessary, maybe, but soulless; they can't be trusted.

This guy – we'll call him Engelbert – no, too much fun in that, let's call him Norman – turned up the day after the fire, asking questions like, 'Did you fit the log burner?' and so on. Adam had done everything properly, but it looked at first as though the insurance company wouldn't pay out because they said, as it was commercial accommodation, he should have had the log burner installed by a specialist company and signed off, and he hadn't – he'd done it himself. Adam explained that when he was first converting the bus it was intended just for himself and his daughter to use. Norman said, 'Well, that would be alright if it's true, but we've only got your word for it. How could we possibly know?'

'Well, how about a recording of me saying that, on a programme that was aired on national television and seen by millions of people?' said Adam. So there. Norman seemed a bit deflated, thanks to Plum Pictures.

That was December 2019, and with the help of friends like David, Andy, myself, Simon and Clementine, and his sister Nadia and brother-in-law Nick, he was up and running again by the spring. We were all sanding, painting and cheering Adam up while he removed ruined windows and scorched wood, and got on with the rebuild. Simon and I lent him cash for materials while he waited for the insurance company to shuffle through their sloth-like processes, so he could get on with getting his business back online and earning.

This time, he fireproofed to the nth degree, well beyond official requirements. He was determined that, even allowing for human error, like guests overstuffing the burner with wood or leaving it unattended while alight – don't do that, kids, wherever you're staying – it wouldn't cause a fire again. By the time he was done, the bus looked even better than before, and this time everything was signed off to a commercial standard.

Adam was delighted to open up in April 2020, only for Covid to hit hard. It was a bit on and off after that, as for everyone else in hospitality, and there wasn't much to be done about it. Even when movement wasn't restricted, people were less inclined to book a stay somewhere and risk the contact rules changing again.

Devon and Adam made the most of it, spending the summer lockdown at the bus as a change from the flat. That meant they got a little of the original plan in the end – him and his girl, hanging out, sort of on holiday, although of course for many people it was such a terrible time. It was a great place to stay, especially as it was all brand new upstairs, but they couldn't make plans as it was so unclear what was going to happen. Adam was imagining a zombie apocalypse type of affair.

Every so often, they'd return to Brighton to collect mail and it was deeply odd: no buses for a start. No tourists, no students, quiet roads. There was an air of risking life and limb to get supplies. Once they were allowed out to exercise, Adam remembers evenly spaced people of every age, shape and size braving Lycra on the seafront to escape the claustrophobia, looking a bit earnest and crazed. It was indeed like a zombie apocalypse, mashed up with the dance video for local lad Fatboy Slim's hit 'Praise You' by Spike Jonze and Roman Coppola. Adam and Devon kept their visits brief: get the post, pick up food on the way back, escape back to the bus.

The bus venture was a limited company, so business rates had to be paid. Fortunately, the government gave financial support for the leisure industry during the pandemic, which helped make up for the lost income. Adam opened the bus briefly once it was permitted, but his heart wasn't in it really. It was hard not to feel a bit jaded after Covid and he didn't want to do it anymore. He thought about selling it and tried briefly, but the bus itself wasn't worth much, even though it was well known and made money.

However, there wasn't much else he could do with the site, as his planning conditions were so specific. He had to have a bus, and it had to be green, oddly. He was allowed very little lighting, to avoid bothering the bats. There was to be no noise past 11 at night, or anything amplified. All understandable restrictions for the sake of the wildlife and the neighbours, but pretty limiting. He persuaded himself to buckle down and give it five more years and managed to get motivated again. Investing some more money, he bought a new wood-fired hot tub, refreshed the plants and opened up in spring 2022.

It's a Knockout

But then disaster struck again: another fire, despite all his precautions.

This fire, nearly two and a half years later in April 2022 was much bigger and it started downstairs. Again, there were no casualties, but it changed everything permanently. The guests were a family of British influencers with many millions of followers between them, who'd initially tried to get the stay as a freebie. Adam didn't go for it, explaining to them that it wasn't really necessary as the bus just did its thing. Perhaps that put their noses out of joint a bit, but they booked anyway.

Adam welcomed the family and showed them around, and it all seemed to start off well. They called him later saying they had an issue with the boiler, so he popped over to see what the problem was. It turned out to be human error, as it so often is, but these things happen of course when you're a guest somewhere and you don't know how things work. When he arrived at the bus at about ten in the morning, they were sitting having breakfast in their nightclothes. He restarted the boiler and explained about the button that turns the boiler off, which had been pressed. He suggested they not press it. On his way out, he saw smoke rising from the fire pit area and smelt something savoury – sausages, he thought at the time, and commented as he left.

Returning from his errands, he noticed that the family's car was gone, and it looked as though they'd all gone out. Adam was due to have a Ménière's-related operation that day, which involved injecting steroids into his ear. They start by dripping in liquid local anaesthetic, hoovering it back out a few minutes later. Once they've punched two holes in your eardrum, they squirt steroids through one of them into the middle ear. Your job is to lie still, trying not to talk, swallow or yawn while the steroids reach the inner ear by absorption through the round window membrane. It's hideous and very painful, but about half the time it kick-starts temporary relief, at least from vertigo and instability, so there's a mix of dread and hope beforehand.

Adam was about to leave for his appointment when all the alarms went off in the shed by the entrance to the bus site. That's where he kept his tools and beekeeping equipment, and it's where the solar panels were mounted as they're a bit unsightly. The alarm is usually triggered because someone on the bus has plugged in something too powerful, like hair straighteners. To reset the alarm, Adam turned off the power to the bus and then turned it back on, but it immediately triggered the alarm again. He looked up and saw smoke billowing up into the air from the direction of the bus, and he ran down there thinking 'Oh no! Not again!'

The fire was on an epic scale this time. The whole front of the bus was aflame, and the fire was massively hot, popping and banging, with windows exploding. Adam couldn't understand it. All there was at the front of the bus was the old driver's cabin; the electrics for the kitchen, the cooker and the wood burner were all further back. There was nothing obvious that could catch fire there, except with the help of something that's already very hot.

It was phenomenally loud, this fire, roaring and crackling. Shouting to his partner Enfys to call the fire brigade, Adam ran round to the back of the bus to try to move the LPG gas bottle away from the heat. If you've ever seen an LPG gas bottle explode you'll know it isn't funny; if the bottles had exploded they would likely have killed him and anyone on the bus. This incident plays on Adam's mind even now, haunts him a little, the cracking noise and the confusion.

So, while he was working to get the bottles, already troublingly warm, well away from the bus, and trying to avoid inhaling smoke or getting burned, Enfys looked for her phone. In the panic, she couldn't find it, so she used Adam's phone, and the next thing he knows there is a voice in his head is asking, 'What service do you require?' He assumes it's Enfys and yells, 'Call the ****ing fire brigade!'

Ménière's gradually erodes your hearing, so Adam uses these amazing hearing aids, the best in the world. They're very sophisticated, unlike standard NHS ones. They're Bluetooth enabled, so calls come straight through, since he wouldn't notice a normal phone ring. It suddenly dawned on him in his panic that that's what had happened. Enfys couldn't hear anything on his phone because the voice of the emergency services was coming straight through to his ear, so she wasn't saying anything to them. The emergency services couldn't hear anything because, although he was yelling, he was too far from the phone and Enfys for either of them to hear him. It was chaos.

He went back to Enfys and sorted out the situation, and then they called the guests just to make sure no one needed rescuing. They discovered the whole family was safely out and about in their car. Adam went to see if he could fight the fire, but it was impossible, and the bus was starting to fill with thick, black smoke.

The fire was so bad that it took the fire brigade nearly eight hours to put out the blaze. Buses are made of lightweight aluminium, which melts at a

The front of the burnt bus

relatively low temperature, so every time they put the fire out, molten metal fell on the wooden decking and set it aflame again. The front driver's side tyre was burning too, which doesn't happen easily. Tyre fires are difficult to extinguish once they start and they produce thick, dark smoke full of toxins like cyanide, carbon monoxide and sulphur dioxide.

The firefighters were great, but their job is to work as fast as they can – they aren't shy about smashing windows to get hoses in, so they and their water destroyed anything the fire hadn't already consumed. It was inevitable,

The charred interior of the bus

but gutting to watch. If it hadn't been so upsetting seeing something he loved burn, Adam would have been fascinated to see how they work. He used to want to be in the fire brigade – drawn to large vehicles from early on – and he applied a couple of times in his late twenties but unsuccessfully. Then he hit 30, after which age they didn't recruit, though there's no upper age limit now due to age discrimination laws. Anyway, at the bus, the crew had placed a board with numbers on, corresponding to the number each firefighter had on his or her jacket, so that the crew chief would know if a firefighter was left inside.

CSI Sussex

The bus was completely and utterly destroyed. Adam had to phone the family and tell them not to come back, that he was sorry but the bus and everything in it was gone, so any possessions they hadn't taken with them were lost forever. Understandably, they weren't happy and wanted to come and get the things they'd left behind. Adam asked them to give him a list of what was missing, and said he'd go and look once he was allowed to re-enter after the loss adjuster had visited. The dad was asking Adam how he thought the fire had started and whether it was an electrics issue, which Adam thought was odd. Then he was asking him to imagine if his kids had been in there, and saying the bus was unsafe. Adam said there was no indication of it having been unsafe yet – that it may just have been an accident, but they had to wait for the report.

The next morning, it was loss adjuster time, and guess who it was. Yes, only your friend and mine, Norman. Now, he was an old guy and maybe that's why he was like he was, just ground down, but there was no empathy there at all. Adam was still clearly in shock, his livelihood literally in ashes, and Norman was making jokes, telling him about his dog, just not reading the room. Perhaps it was well intentioned but, even as Adam continued to look glum, it escalated to the point that Norman was relating his exploits as a teenager in the sixties. Adam realises now he was probably clumsily trying to find a connection and empathise, but at the time it was a very surreal experience. Eventually, he got to the point and said they needed a forensics team to come and establish the cause. Adam wondered whether this was adjuster-speak for trying to find something he'd done wrong as an excuse for the company not to pay out. Thankfully, however, the insurer agreed that everything was in order and properly signed-off. The basic claim took nearly a year to resolve of course, but finally Adam heard from Norman that he would be paid in full for his insured losses – a very nice birthday present.

It was strange though, because according to the forensics report the fire seemed to have started around the driver's seat area, or underneath it, and it concluded that the cause of the fire must be an electrical issue. Adam explained that all the wires around that area were a legacy from when it was a passenger bus – the wires went into a fuse box behind the seat but there was no longer any power to them. However, the insurance company was adamant.

They must have had some doubt though because they sent a senior forensics person next, who looked more carefully. She said it seemed almost as though the fire had started underneath the bus. She went through bins, taking photographs. She studied cigarette butts found on the drive and in the flower pots, and a rectangular burn on a bench Adam had made out of sleepers, by the fire pit, a few metres away. When her report came through, it suggested the cause of the fire could have been cigarettes or could have been electrical. Adam still felt this was wrong.

He decided to get his own forensics expert in, both for his peace of mind and to protect himself. Emma Wilson, a director at Prometheus Forensic Services, came to the site and noticed that a metal skillet, which had been placed over the bench burn, was bigger than the burn itself, so couldn't have been its cause. Enfys had actually flagged this up to Adam on the day of the fire, but in all the chaos he'd forgotten about that. She reminded him with great indignation when he told her what Emma had said.

Emma recognised the burn mark as coming from a disposable barbecue. These things are a menace: they only cost a couple of quid but they cause loads of trouble, setting fire to bins after people have thoughtlessly chucked them, burning grass and so on. People have been trying to get them banned for years.

Emma measured the burn mark, consulted her records and found that the dimensions matched only one specific type of small disposable barbecue. If they could find evidence of one of those, they'd be getting somewhere, but there was no sign at first. The previous investigators had already been through the metal pedal bin in the kitchen, the plastic inner sleeve of which had melted in the heat and then set as a black disc right at the bottom of the bin.

Emma pushed this plastic patty; it plopped out, and there it was underneath – a perfectly preserved wrapper from a Co-op disposable barbecue, the very type she had identified. She put together a possible scenario, and wondered whether the remains of the barbecue had been put under the front of the bus by the wheel, where the fire had started. There was no sign at first, which didn't surprise her as she predicted that all trace of the aluminium tray would have melted. However, she said it was worth looking for the grate, as they're made of steel. Steel needs more than double the temperature of aluminium to melt, more than three times the heat needed to burn tyres. She looked around and it wasn't long before she found a big cowpat of melted aluminium by the front driver's-side wheel. She levered it up, and underneath was the perfectly preserved steel grate. She took photographs as evidence.

However, when asked about the barbecue, the guests denied it. Maybe what happened was something like this: they noticed that, by accident, they'd burnt the bench, and felt embarrassed. Had they called Adam at this point, he'd have asked them not to smoke or use disposable barbecues at the site, as they're hazards, and told them not to worry about the bench as he could easily sand the mark away or simply turn it over. Everyone makes mistakes and most likely no harm was meant.

Instead, perhaps they panicked, hid the offending barbecue on the wooden decking that tucked under the front driver's side of the bus without fully extinguishing it, and went off on a day trip. Meanwhile, it slowly set fire to something – leaves, twigs or the decking, perhaps – which caused a big enough fire right next to the front tyre so that in time whoosh! Once the tyre caught, the fire would have been out of control and impossible to put out until it had destroyed everything.

The legal duty of full and frank disclosure meant Adam had to tell the insurance company about the findings. The company asked to see the forensics report he'd commissioned, and they were impressed. They said that, on the basis of the report, they were going to take the family to court themselves, to cover their losses. If an insurance company decides to do that, it means you can't do the same. The company offered to pay for the report – 1,700 quid – but there were still legal costs Adam had to cover and there was nothing he could do about it. If he didn't comply with the company, there would be no more payouts and a lot of uninsured loss.

As is standard procedure, the family then had the chance to send their own forensics expert to site. In the meantime, the father was phoning Adam repeatedly, very angry. He listed thousands of pounds' worth of personal possessions that he alleged had been in the bus. Adam had to get his solicitor to write to the father to get him to stop, since they weren't supposed to be communicating directly. It was pretty horrific.

The family did hire their own forensics expert, but it took months before they'd finished their investigation. Until then, he could do nothing else with the site. That wasn't great, as his loss of earnings cover only lasted for 12 months, and time was already ticking. On a more positive note, the insurance company did eventually agree that Adam could tag some of his uninsured losses onto the back of their claim against the family.

Another significant loss was the coveted place in the Google rankings that the Big Green Bus had earned over time. The bus used to sell out a season in advance, but trying to start a business from zero is quite another matter in the competitive marketplace of online holiday bookings.

The Kindness of Strangers

When news spread about the fire, Adam was contacted by a guest, Mick, who'd visited the bus with his family. Mick explained that his son Rob had been a keen mechanic who'd built his own car. Rob had watched the build on TV and had wanted to come to stay at the bus but sadly hadn't made it as he had died – far too young.

Instead, Mick had visited with the rest of his family, as part of a memorial tour of various places his son had liked, even ones he hadn't had the chance to visit. Most were related to vehicles or mechanics, like Silverstone and Brands Hatch. They had buried a trail of specially engraved sockets from his son's favourite socket set as they went, and had planted one under the front bumper of the bus some time ago.

He asked Adam to keep the socket if he found it and incorporate it into whatever came next. Mick understood it must be the last thing on Adam's mind, but actually it became a bit of an obsession for him. Unfortunately, the front of the bus was where the worst damage was, and the most water. Adam looked carefully, once he was allowed to disturb the site, but had no luck. Even a massive magnet, the kind you use in rivers, was no help (the bus was mostly non-magnetic aluminium, so that wouldn't interfere with the search). He found all sorts of rubbish, but not the socket, sadly.

Once he'd contacted Mick to explain, he received a replacement one in the post, engraved 'Rob's sockets: A tribute to a legend, through the distribution of a toolkit.' An online book of remembrance listed the locations where the family had hidden the sockets, all over the country – the bus was location number 1.

This is just one example – the most poignant perhaps – of how much the bus meant to so many people. Adam believes that at least one child was conceived on the bus too – his friend Tom's daughter Harriet, although his partner Natalie disputes that. Not to speak of the life of the bus before he owned it! People even came to stay on the bus who had once driven it when it was in service. It brought a lot of happiness to many people – that's the nice thing about being involved in people's holidays.

After the first fire, friends had rallied round and turned up in person to help clean the place up, rebuild and repaint, which cheered Adam up and kept him going. Everyone would hang out, cook on the barbecue and have a nice day. This time was different. Not only was the site closed for insurance reasons but the bus was way too far gone for them to even try to repair it. That made it a lonelier experience.

However, there was still plenty of support, not only from patrons who'd stayed at the bus but from total strangers. One lovely bloke wrote him this message:

> *'I'm still gutted you have lost the bus, I'm from Coventry so may of even travelled to school/college or just about the city on it with my parents. Just nice to still see it having a use instead of scrapped. I hope you can recover from this and just like Coventry itself, raise from the ashes!'*

I love the fact that people take the trouble to try and cheer you up, when they don't even know you. People sent lovely photos of their children in the driving seat of the bus, or rolling about on the bunks, to keep Adam's spirits up. Here are extracts for a few more of the messages he received at the time, to give you a taste of how it felt.

> *'The green phoenix will rise again! I smashed my converted camper up last year, so I know how it feels. Keep going matey.'*

> *'If anyone can, you can Adam! Do you have a fundraiser page? I'd happily donate xx.'*

'You often appear in conversation as the person I know with the most bravery, determination, innovation, creativity and the driving will to see it all through – especially in the face of adversity. Something extraordinary will arise from this...'

'Six years ago since I took my missus to The Big Green Bus for her 30th. We talk about it EVERY year. We had hurricanes, lots of booze, amazing chilli (another post asking for you to sell the spice mix please) and lots of memories – thanks Adam!'

'We miss her very much, we always wanted to bring our kids to stay on the bus, but perhaps we'll bring them to the new venture instead :)'

'Can't wait to see the progress shots on this new project! The BGB lives on in the memories and photos of those lucky enough to have stayed in her.'

'This was my favourite bus in service in Coventry 2464 so gutted and upset I was and still am and I also feel for u too but I will remember travelling on this bus and I'm so looking forward to ur next chapter RIP.'

One rather lovely thing that happened was that Mike, who'd sold him the bus in the first place, got in touch. Having heard about the fire, he offered Adam another bus for nothing. Though that was very kind and Adam massively appreciated the thought, he didn't take up the offer. He thought people wouldn't feel the same about coming to stay on a bus so much if it wasn't the famous one from TV. He's been offered three free buses in total – aren't people amazing?

However, it wouldn't have been possible to take Mike up on his offer even if he wanted to. When he first installed the bus on the site, it was driven in through neighbouring land that had since been built on, as the main entrance is too narrow to turn a vehicle with that length of wheelbase. There's no access for a double-decker any more.

Stealthy Escape

The second fire was in April 2020, but it was anyone's guess how long he'd have to wait before he could take the bus remains off the land, let alone replace it, and till then he'd be paying rates and managing normal living costs without any income.

Had things been different, he might have relocated to France at this point, but of course Brexit had kiboshed that possibility since he bought the house in Limousin. Suddenly, it had become difficult and expensive to take furniture and materials over (it was now cheaper to buy things in France), so finishing the work became even harder. Also, rule changes meant it was too expensive to take Salbo – companion and, if pushed, guard dog – with him anymore, and it looked like they wouldn't be allowed to live over there either.

Adam thought about what he could sell, but all that was left was the land the burnt bus was on, which couldn't be touched for now, an old van no longer needed for travelling to France, and his home – a two-bed flat in Brighton with a hefty mortgage that was becoming unaffordable with all the fire trouble. He started with the flat. Devon had headed off to university long since, so didn't need her bedroom. He made a few inexpensive changes to make it less like a bachelor pad and more suitable for a family, so that it would fetch a little more on the rental market. This seemed a perfect solution, except for one tiny detail: it meant he had nowhere to live.

The van he'd been using for France was a Luton, which is the sort with the driver's cab separate and a box on the back. There's also a small section over the cab. Rather than selling it, he converted it so that he'd have somewhere to live while renting out the flat. Vehicles to the rescue, once again! He'd been following a group on social media where people shared ideas about converting Luton vans, and was quite taken with them. It seemed to him that the van was just sitting there, crying out to become a camper. Come to think of it, that's how many vehicles look to Adam: ripe for conversion. Perhaps, with that religious education CSE, he should have joined the Church after all.

With the income generated by renting out the flat, he used a similar approach to the one he had taken to convert the bus, but on a smaller scale, and, again, reclaimed materials were the order of the day. He was relieved to find that the work was easy compared with adapting the bus: a regular, modern, rectangular void with nice, straight walls is much less trouble than a double-decker's curves and tapers.

Also, unlike the bus, he wanted to make this into a 'stealth' camper. A stealth camper can be parked in a place overnight without being seen as anything other than a plain old van. They've become increasingly popular, thanks in part to them being less attractive to thieves than a conspicuous camper. Given his financial situation, Adam thought he might need to do a bit of that to get through this difficult period, plus it felt ninja-sneaky, which made it more fun. This van had three rooflights, but no windows in the sides, and the whole back wall was a vertical shutter.

Now he's converted it, when you push up the rear shutter, you see a wooden stable door mounted in a wall with a window. It has its own 12-volt system for power, which charges up when you drive along. There are leisure batteries to power the fridge, TV and lights. It has solar panels on the roof, and at a paid campsite you can access its electric hook-up points. He fitted two water tanks underneath – one for fresh water and the other for grey, so that you could use clean water to wash your mug, for example, then store the dirty water until it's possible to dispose of it responsibly.

The most difficult part of the Luton conversion was cutting a large enough cavity in the back of the driver's cab and the front wall of the box so that his partner Enfys and he could crawl from one to the other, without attracting attention to themselves by getting out and pulling up the whole shutter at the back. He went to enormous trouble to do this, because a secret house hidden inside a shabby exterior has irresistible, Tardis-like appeal, with a side order of glamorous espionage. Guess how often they actually needed to be stealthy, after all that...

He built a shower and installed a chemical toilet for ablutions, with a cosy king-size bed over the cab, and a sofa bed in the main section for relaxing. The kitchen area had a gas hob and oven, sink and fall-proof shelving. It was well insulated and he took the time to make it attractive too, which helped to take his mind off the fire.

Although he did everything himself, it only took six weeks to complete. Once he and Enfys had moved in, they parked it on the bus site, near the entrance. The trouble was that the whole area still stank of the fire, especially when it rained, which was a constant reminder of the damage and the frustrating tedium of waiting for a resolution. The cordoned-off husk of the bus was still there in all its skeletal misery, and he wasn't allowed to clear it up. The helplessness didn't feel great. It wasn't yet clear what the outcome would be: whether he'd still have a livelihood at the end of it, and what on earth he'd replace the bus with. As soon as he didn't have the van conversion to distract him, the situation started to get him down.

One morning he woke up, turned to Enfys and said, 'Let's go.'

'Where?'

'Road trip.'

They started planning. The idea was to go to the little house in France, stay there a couple of weeks, then follow their noses around Europe. They got Salbo her Brexit medical so that they could take her with them. This meant she was certificated to spend four months in Europe at a time, although humans only get three. Croatia wasn't part of the Eurozone until 2023, so they planned to make their way there after a couple of months and get their passports stamped to stop the clock on their three Eurozone months until they recrossed the border. Then they'd have a month left to make their way home.

They had a good time at the French house, then headed south to hang out in the French Riviera, crossed into Italy for a bit, made for Lake Garda and even stretched to a lobster birthday dinner for Enfys. This was all paid for by seasonal work picking grapes in vineyards as they went, topped up with what was left over from the flat rental once the mortgage was paid. Next came Slovenia, and more vineyards, before they crossed into Croatia.

Hitting the road in the converted Luton van

Enfys and Salbo relax on the camper's front porch

They had a few problems there. The van was pretty heavy, loaded down with their possessions, water and so on. On the winding roads of the Croatian countryside, this put quite a strain on the machine. Once, they heard a huge bang as they were driving. Adam pulled over to check but couldn't see any cause for alarm.

Later, coming back to the van from the loo at their campsite, Adam noticed the van was sagging at the back. Investigation showed the leaf spring had completely snapped in two. He drove the van, very carefully, to a Renault garage – the wheel was only about an inch shy of the wheel arch. The garage couldn't deal with it though, as it was too heavy for their ramps. They sent him to an HGV garage, so he crawled there with his fingers crossed. The people there were very helpful and ordered the parts, saying they could fix it the next day. They didn't even mind that Adam and Enfys had to sleep in it till then. They fixed the problem, charged a reasonable price and sent them on their way the following afternoon.

Adam and Enfys intended to spend a month in Croatia, but stayed longer because it was so beautiful. The beachside campsite they stayed at, out of season by this time, was quiet and calm. There was a heatwave, so it was still warm late in the year at Rabac, a small coastal town on the Istrian peninsula. It's on the eastern side, so not as well known as the resorts on the western side, but it has clean water, shingle beaches and mountainous views. During their travels, wherever they went, every other morning Adam would wake up, look up a route for a run of six miles or so and head out on his own. He'd pick a different direction each time so that he got to explore the whole area. Salbo would stay and keep Enfys company, less keen on the long runs than she used to be.

Adam puts his feet up after a day's work in the vineyard

Around this time, Plum Pictures showed serious interest in filming the next conversion. In fact, they even decided to film the eventual demolition of the bus, to link it to the Season 2 show about the bus, and all this before they'd even had series 12 confirmed by Channel 4. Adam's head started to clear, letting him consider the future. He did a lot of thinking on his morning runs, and it was after one of these that he texted me. I usually write fiction, but he asked whether I'd still be interested in turning the whole story into a book, as I'd suggested years ago.

Coastal campervanning in Croatia

After six weeks in Croatia, Adam and Enfys felt it was time to head home, so they drove back via the Swiss Alps. They'd been away for over four months in total; in the midst of disaster and with a low budget, they'd ended up having the trip of a lifetime. Adam was especially grateful because when you're running a holiday rental you can't afford to ignore your business long enough to have a holiday of this duration, so the trip was a silver lining to having no business for a while.

He'd been taking a few meetings online while they were away, with the bank, the insurance company and the council planning department. It was finally starting to look like the bus could be moved soon. They got home in December to find an email to say he could remove the bus. He was very glad not to have spent eight months waiting for that news while staring at a dead bus and scorched site, waking up to the stench of smoke every morning.

Still very short of funds, when his neighbour in France messaged him, offering to buy his house for 30,000 euros, he agreed. Adam didn't really want to sell but decided it was better to raise money for the next build, foreseeing a long road ahead with the cabin. He made a little money on the sale, although there was tax to pay and he'd invested a lot of hope and time, as well as the caravan full of tools he'd left there, and the plans. At least he had saved the house from crumbling into the ground. You can't win 'em all.

Clean Slate

The fact that the neighbouring land was more developed than when he first bought the woods for the bus meant that he would have to demolish the once-green, now-black bus on site and remove it piecemeal. This would take money and time. He and Enfys were still living in the van, which was comfortable and warm, but a bit of a tight squeeze for two adults and a medium-sized dog, especially through the winter when you're indoors more of the time.

He got a nasty shock when the quotes came in for taking the bus apart and disposing of it. It looked like it would cost a stunning £10,000 minimum. That was out of the question, so he started working out how to do it himself. He bought a JCB (new big-vehicle toy!) to drag the heavy bits of bus about. Even the JCB couldn't tow the weight of the whole chassis at once though, so he had to buy hydraulic cutters to chop it in half. These are heavy-duty, hand-held cutters known as 'jaws of life', used by fire officers to extricate people from wrecked cars in motorway pile-ups.

He managed to cut the massive chassis in half, but even then it was still seriously heavy. The only way the JCB could drag it towards the gate was if he put all the stands down and pulled it a metre, then lifted the stands, moved the JCB forwards one metre and repeated the process. It took all day, like a very elderly but determined giant scorpion dragging prey to its lair.

Dismantling the bus was surprisingly difficult – nearly as hard as building it, and much more depressing. He was sad to be taking his own creation apart, and conditions were tough: it was snowing, it was the coldest December in a decade, the winter days were short and he often had to work in little light. Everything was heavy and his back hurt. It was grim.

Having taken the aluminium off – the remains of the roof, upstairs floor and ground floor walls – he pulled up the plywood on the ground floor, leaving the metal chassis and wheels. He removed some air tanks, panels and a few other bits and pieces and gave them to someone else working on an identical model of bus. The air tanks have now been transplanted into a brother bus, which will extend its life for a few more years.

Adam managed to get about £4,000 for the aluminium reclaimed from the site, the engine, the rear wheels and gearbox, and some rare panels such as those over the wheel arches. All this matter, this metal, whose assembly had made the bus a real thing that played a small part in many people's lives, was now being disassembled and dispersed. He felt better knowing that much of it was being recycled and would have another use. Despite appearances, there was a little green spirit left in that old black hulk.

Winter rolls around

Removing the ruins with the JCB

He had to pay for skips to take away the waste, but even so, after buying then reselling the JCB and jaws of life, he was about a thousand pounds in credit, not allowing for all the time and effort it took. Adam was pretty pleased with himself for being £11,000 better off than if he'd paid someone else to do the work, plus he didn't get rid of the JCB till he'd used it to shift about the materials for the new build. This 'buy it, use it, sell it' approach has served him well over the years.

On 27 January 2023, the last of the old burnt bus left the site, apart from the few mementoes Adam kept safe to incorporate into a future build.

- 7 -
Phoenix
Starting something even better

Challenge Accepted

Adam had thought the original bus build was tough, but he'd found the little van quite easy, so imagined this next build would be fine. He was totally unprepared for the fact that it would be much, much harder. There were several reasons for this.

Emotionally, the journey was very different. The bus idea evolved gradually from a personal whim, a light-hearted project with his young daughter, into a more professional affair. It sprang from his usual impulsive sense of fun and blind enthusiasm, and there wasn't much pressure on him, apart from some shooting deadlines once TV got involved.

This time, by contrast, he had less agency: he could pick the details of what he built, but he had no choice overall – he needed to replace the income, as he had a mortgage to pay. It also felt like a less personal project, as he now had a limited company. Not only that: he had much less time, because the financial pressure created time pressure, so he had to apply for planning permission not long after the fire. The bus had been a long time in the planning and making, by comparison.

In terms of morale, the fire wasn't his fault, but the investigation made him feel suspected. He was also uncomfortable with the fact that those who seemed responsible, although of course it wasn't deliberate, weren't accepting liability, which delayed resolution. Like everyone else, he'd been through the Covid years, and like many he'd been hit hard by Brexit, since it affected his house in France as well as the hospitality industry in the UK.

Physically, he was a decade older, more deaf and feeling less able to do full-time carpentry to earn extra money. On top of all that, the glamping industry had changed. He'd got used to the bus and its self-maintaining popularity and fame, but he'd been lucky with his timing first time round. The market is busier now, with a yurt, shepherd's hut or bus round every corner. Covid boosted the staycation market, but developed it too, so he needed to push the boundaries again, look into the future, keep it fresh.

The few negatives he'd received in the bus feedback over the years concerned the temperature in winter. To keep warm, guests needed to invest time feeding the log burner, and some people didn't want to spend their holiday doing that. Others struggled to light or maintain the fire, so couldn't raise the temperature enough. The bus was at heart a seasonal business. It appealed to young children and families, so school holidays and weekends sold out fast, but winter weekdays were much less popular. This was partly because, as businesses like Airbnb grew, it had become easier and cheaper to rent a family-friendly place, perhaps by the sea.

If Adam wanted to make something that could compete in this new marketplace he needed to think differently, creating something more modern and comfortable that could keep guests happy and warm all year round. He won't really know if he's succeeded in that until after a year of trading, when vacancy rates and reviews for a whole year of rentals for the bus and the cabin can be compared, but early signs are good. It wasn't the easiest option to go a little more high end, but if he was going to make something to last, and appeal in a more crowded market, he needed to make it as good as he possibly could.

The physical labour was tough: he found everything heavy, *really* heavy, and awkwardly shaped. Every day consisted of working till it got dark, trudging back to the van, eating and sleeping, exhausted. Enfys warned that he'd make himself ill, but he still put a lot of pressure on himself. After he'd finished the cabin, he told her, he'd forget how hard it had been, how he could barely get himself out of bed. Once in the swing of it, he enjoyed part of every day, but sometimes felt angry, tired and on the verge of giving up. Having the TV deadline, a bit of external accountability, gave him something to focus on and helped with motivation.

Giving up wasn't really an option. If he didn't make it work, the bank was going to foreclose on the mortgage Adam had on the land, and he would lose everything. It was anyone's guess how much the insurance company would eventually cough up, because they were keeping him in the dark, which wasn't what the bank wanted to hear. The land on its own wasn't worth much – certainly less than the value of the mortgage. What he needed to build was a more permanent, less mobile structure that would dramatically increase the value of the land, so it didn't feel like a money pit.

Many trades and suppliers let him down during the build – they were all having a hard time in a difficult economic climate too, of course. Guy the plumber and Rob the electrician, both of whom had worked on the bus, were brilliant though. Enfys got stuck in as well, doing all kinds of horrible jobs without complaint. So, all in all, it felt like a huge challenge, but he buckled down and got through it in five and a half months: quite a pace compared with the bus.

Back to the Drawing Board

Adam managed to get a loan for £20,000 while waiting for the insurance payout. Plum Pictures, the TV company that filmed him before, came along to film the demolition of the bus as part of the context for filming the new build for series 12 of *Amazing Spaces*. This was a real morale boost and a huge relief, as Adam hoped the publicity he'd receive when the new series aired would help to jumpstart the new business, and he knew from experience that the deadlines would be useful, though they would be stressful too. It all helped him to stop mourning and look forwards.

Having established that he couldn't get the bus off the site intact, let alone another bus onto it, ruled out a like-for-like replacement. At first, he had no idea what to do next, but realised that it would have to be very different. Fire engines had come onsite quite easily during the fire, so he knew that a vehicle smaller than the bus would work. However, it's good from a planning point of view to replace a previous structure that had been granted planning permission with one of a similar size, because if you go smaller it's hard to scale back up at a later date.

Also, he thought the replacement would need to offer at least as much accommodation, since the bank was breathing down his neck and the business needed to be able to turn over at least as much as it had when he had the bus. He thought it would have to sleep at least six people like the bus did, to enable him to make enough money to repay his loans. Thanks in part to Plum Pictures, ironically, a lot of the possibilities didn't seem very exciting anymore, as anyone interested in turning unconventional things into places to live had already seen other people do that on programmes like *Amazing Spaces*.

Adam had to come up with something new, something modular, that could go in the space left by the bus. After some thought, he hit on the idea of building a house out of shipping containers. So-called cargotecture has been on the rise for a while, and it already wasn't that unusual to convert single containers, but multiples were less common. Stacked containers have been used successfully in cities, like at the Southbank branch of Wahaca, and 88 of them make up eco-friendly Buck Street Market in Camden, which looks great. There still aren't many in use as holiday homes in the UK though, so this had a chance of feeling as fresh as the bus had in its heyday.

Containers are about eight feet wide but come in various lengths: 10, 20 or 40 feet long. The 40-footers were too long to get onto the site, and the 10-footers would have been too small to offer enough accommodation, but the 20-footers were just right – a Goldilocks-perfect size. Four of these containers together would be a similar total size to the bus, though each part would be much smaller. Adam calculated that a specialised vehicle with rear-steering axles could just about reverse onto the land to deliver the containers.

If he'd just had a replacement bus, no new planning permission would have been needed, but changing tack meant running the gauntlet of the planning department again, which filled him with anxiety. It had been very unpleasant the first time around, so he dreaded it. It felt like quite a hill to climb, but he

couldn't see an alternative. He got some plans drawn up for the cabin and submitted them to the council, then crossed his fingers and prayed to Fortuna.

It took a while to get any payment out of the insurance company, and for the first year everything they gave him was 'on account', meaning they'd claw it back if they ended up feeling he was responsible for the fire in any way, which added to the stress. His first payment didn't arrive till June 2022 and some of that had to be spent on gaining planning permission.

Most of the rest of it went on repaying the guests who'd lost out due to the fire. He didn't have to, you might argue, as people could claim on their own travel insurance in this sort of situation, but it didn't feel right. He also hoped that people would rebook in the cabin, though that hasn't really happened so far. To give him a clear conscience and feel better going forwards, it was important.

There was still no news about the planning consent. He kept social media going and slowly started to build a new brand identity for the cabin. Keeping the basic shape and feel of the logo exactly the same to suggest continuity, he replaced the image of the bus with an image of the cabin. This image was taken from the plans he'd submitted to the council: it shows the cabin at the same jaunty angle as the bus had been, which foregrounds its round end-windows. Devon's boyfriend, Jack Olley, made the finished design and people seemed to like it.

Around this time, the planning application sailed through without a hitch, and Adam's spirits started to return to their usual 'how hard can it be' level. Things were really looking up.

D. Page Contractors with one of their eight mighty helical piles

Screw Ups

As off-grid homes, both the bus and the cabin count as pretty green, with electricity for lighting and sockets powered by solar panels, and LPG gas canisters for cooking food and heating water. LPG is a fossil fuel, which isn't ideal, but it's considered low carbon because it emits no black carbon and far less CO_2 than coal and oil. The bus had a log burner as well, whereas the cabin has LPG-fuelled central heating. This time, however, there was no concrete involved in the build.

Instead of concrete, there are eight very impressive ground screws, or 'helical piles' thanks to specialists D. Page Contractors Ltd, who gave Adam a great deal and were real professionals. First, he needed to take precise measurements for the container bases so that when they arrived they could be lifted straight onto the mountings like they are on ships, because the weight is all borne in the corners. Once the area has been checked to avoid drilling into pipes or electric cables, a specialist machine drills the screws three metres into the ground, one screw for each corner of each ground-floor container. It's much better for the environment than concrete, and the screws have a long life.

The woodland around the site is mostly planted with pine trees, which are evergreen, and the whole project felt like a continuation in the teeth of difficulties. If the trees can tough out the winter, Adam thought, he could

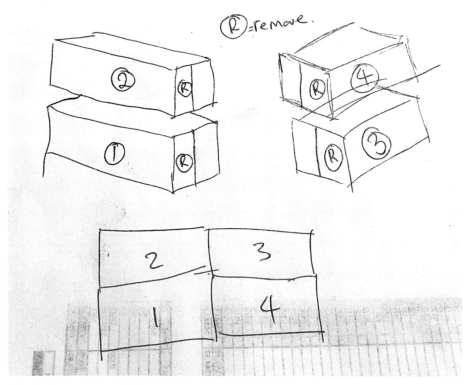

Plan for the sequence of deliveries

rebuild after a fire. Since he planned to convert the containers in an even more eco-conscious way than the bus, he started to think of it as the Evergreen Cabin.

Having organised the water and drainage – such glamorous jobs – it was time to order the containers and book a specialist delivery lorry. The containers would have to be lifted differently from the normal way due to the access to and shape of the site, which necessitated a peculiarly long-reaching crane.

Containers, or sea-boxes as they are also known, have double doors at one end, which open outwards only. The container company agreed to remove half of these before delivery, two left-hand opening ones and two right-hand opening ones. This would create one long room on each storey, with a four-foot-wide opening – half the width of the boxes – in the middle of each storey, without Adam having to cut doorways. The less cutting needed, the better, since these things have thick, corrugated steel walls. This would also mean the outside ends were seriously weatherproof, as they would have no doors.

He then had to make sure the delivery company brought the containers in the right order. They could only bring two at a time, and the two ground floor ones needed to arrive first, and to line up a left-hand door container opposite a right-hand door container, or he would have been in real trouble. The delivery company also needed to place two containers end-to-end like train carriages.

Container 2 with its half-door, waiting to meet container 3

The same thing would need to be done for the upper-floor containers. It took a while before the correct type of lorry had been sourced from a haulage company at the docks, but then they were ready for delivery day.

Adam did warn them not to come if it had been raining hard, or when it was dark, since there was no power at the site, but they ignored that and arrived at 6:30 in the evening in the pouring rain. There was one container on the lorry,

Inspection by peacock

and the second one on a trailer parked in a layby down the road which would be collected once stage one of the delivery had been completed.

For stage one, the truck driver reversed all the way up the drive and managed to deposit the first container in position without too much trouble. Then he drove back to the layby to load up the other container before repeating the process. Unfortunately, stage one must have loosened up the ground, especially in the wet, so this time the truck got deeply stuck. It had hydraulic stabilising arms extending from it, so they put thick wooden sleepers under these to raise the stuck wheels, then Adam tried using the JCB to try to get it out of the rut, but the thing weighed 18 tons and was spinning mud.

It turned out that one of the truck's wheels was stuck on one of the ground screws. They were there for hours in the pouring rain, with the driver swearing furiously and mud spraying everywhere. Then, to make matters worse, the wall of the tyre split. The driver was livid, calling it the worst job ever, but after a couple of hours of sludge and curses they eventually got the truck out. Adam worried the ground screw had been pushed out of position, which would have cost even more and slowed him down, but these screws are too tough to be bothered by a massive crane lorry pirouetting on top of them.

The next two containers were due for delivery by the same Mr Cheerful next morning, so Adam started early and managed to level the ground out a

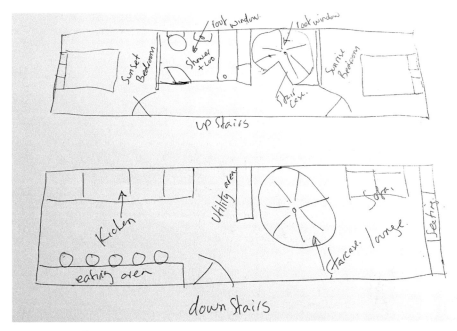

Cabin layout plans

little with the JCB beforehand. With the benefit of sleep and daylight, they managed the second delivery better and the driver was gone by nine o'clock.

Looking up at this monolith, it all felt very sudden and the structure looked enormous – far bigger than the bus. Adam double-checked the plans and container sizes, thinking there'd been a mix-up, but no, it was just huge. It was daunting, but it was a relief to be able to start work at last.

Making Shapes

Hilariously, Adam started off with no way to enter the containers because he'd so carefully had them delivered with the door ends facing one another. He had to somehow find a way to access these boxes from the outside world, and to connect one storey to the other. First, he had to make holes for entry, starting with a two-foot square crawl hole. Even before that, the location of all the doors and windows had to be mapped out, to avoid ending up with a human-sized cat flap in a random place when he'd finished. That took a lot of measuring twice to cut once. He couldn't afford to replace a whole container, especially on the bottom layer, and couldn't have patched the hole up convincingly if he'd messed it up.

He had a metalworker come in and weld everything together and to the ground screws, to make sure the structure was safe and rigid. Usually, you can stack up to nine shipping containers on top of one another, but that's if they're intact. He wasn't sure how they would react structurally to having holes cut

Voids awaiting windows

Cutting the circle for the window cavity

out of them, since their strength comes from being braced and corrugated. It's an elegant, strong and relatively lightweight design, but not if you compromise the structure too much.

A frame of metal girders inside would have been the ideal solution but there wasn't the budget for that. Instead, Adam used his carpentry skills to make a grid of internal wooden studwork to ensure rigidity. First, of course, he had to plan where each room would begin and end, the exact size and height of each window and where the inner doorways would be. Compared with the bus, he had more flexibility, which actually made it harder to decide. Using an angle grinder to cut the holes, he began upstairs for safety reasons; if he did make a mistake, the structure would be less likely to collapse altogether or squash him flat.

It was a good day when the windows arrived. Two of the most expensive things on this build were the containers, at £17,000, and the smart black-framed windows and doors, which were about £10,000. This included the big round windows he was determined to install in the end walls. They're glorious – 1.2 metres in diameter, not like the little portholes you get in boats. Adam didn't want the thing to end up looking like a school portacabin, which is hard to avoid with such a simple rectangular plan and utilitarian materials, so as far as he was concerned these oculus windows were essential. In fact, he chose coiling, curving shapes throughout this build, to create an organic, comfortable environment within its boxy shape – or perhaps to make up for the lack of wheels.

He ended up cursing himself for this though, because cutting round holes in a deep corrugated surface with an angle grinder is not easy and, once you've managed it, you have to build studwork around the curved cavity, which is another challenge. Round window frames are tricky to build. He trimmed these using reclaimed material, working his way round and slowly building a ring out of 26 sections, like a shallow sliver of barrel on its side. Fiddly work.

They look beautiful, and many of the photos he takes of the cabin interior are roundels of tree shadows, sunsets or sunrises projected through these windows and sliding slowly across the wooden walls. To me, they echo the wooden walls of the hot tub outside, and the cochlear curves of the stairs, which would be the next massive job. Adam wanted to connect the two storeys using a spiral staircase; this felt right for something supported entirely by spiral screws.

Having round windows presented a problem as people like privacy in bedrooms. A square blind over a round window would have looked awful. He came up with a solution inspired by how portholes are blacked out in boats – by pushing a round cushion, called a 'bung', into the hole. Adam wanted something slightly more flexible, so he designed a round cushion made of two upholstered semicircular foam pads connected by a fabric hinge. Made by local upholsterer David

Powell, these could be used to block out all the light, or folded down to allow half of it in.

He wanted to use as many second-hand and reclaimed materials in this build as possible – partly to keep costs down but also for ecological reasons and because it's part of the ethos, the history of the bus and the site. One of the tricky things about this is that there's a limit to how far ahead you can plan the design if you're using recycled materials. You can't have a clear image of how it will look from the beginning, as you have to rely on what materials become available.

By chance, his sister saw on Facebook Marketplace that someone was indeed selling a spiral staircase. Adam was sceptical, because it's important to have precisely correct dimensions from the floor level downstairs to the top of the floor upstairs. He needed it to have quite a compact circumference, because containers are narrow, and to be structural – the metal upright post to which all the treads attach, a tall metal collar, had to help support the upper storey.

The one on Facebook was being removed from a stable conversion, and was within a couple of inches of the perfect height. It weighed over a ton and was high quality, so had great structural potential. He went to see it *in situ* before it was removed and took loads of photos. It looked great – a clean, linear design rather than being covered in fancy Victorian twirls like a lot of spiral staircases, so he was relieved when they accepted his offer of £500. He went the next day to collect it and the builders had already disassembled it into piles of nuts and bolts and components, which was brilliant.

He brought it all back and used the many photographs he'd taken to reconstruct the staircase like a giant, three-dimensional jigsaw. Cutting through the roof, across the foot-high gap between the container bodies and into the floor of the upper container was not easy. Surprisingly, a rectangular opening was needed rather than a circular one, and he had bought a plasma cutter for this job, but ended up using the angle grinder as it was easier. It was heavy work, and he had to measure everything repeatedly before cutting out the shape.

He had a few sleepless nights of planning the sequence of jobs, to avoid screwing up or having to redo things. The odds against all this coming together when he'd never done it before were pretty slim, but after a lot of work and a bit of luck, it did.

However, having cut the top of the staircase to fit its new setting, Adam needed to weld the two parts of it together, and bought a welding kit. 'I know,' he thought, having failed to learn his lesson from the bus window debacle, 'I'll get Plum to come and film the welding. How hard can it be?' On the day, a camerawoman turned up to capture his maiden weld. He'd practised sticking random bits of metal together, so he started confidently, talking her through the process as he went, then holding up the joined segment to camera, only for it to come apart in his hands.

'That wasn't supposed to happen, was it?' she said.

The hole for the spiral stairs

The finished staircase

Adam preparing to fit a skylight

'No, no it wasn't,' he snapped. Feeling foolish, Adam tried again, more carefully this time, explaining that they needed to let it cool, demonstrating brushing off the slag, and holding it up to camera for a second time. It came apart of course and he threw a massive strop, telling them to stop filming, that he'd get a bloody welder in to do it. The producer came to ask the camerawoman how it was going and she told him 'He couldn't do it.' The producer was delighted and high-fived her: every TV show needs a little drama.

The size of the staircase determined the upstairs layout. The footprint of the spiral as it came up through the floor determined the size of bedroom one, which was next to it, and he wanted to match those dimensions in the other upstairs container, so that bedroom two became the same size as bedroom one. This in turn dictated the size of the bathroom. It felt to Adam as though the layout should have a degree of symmetry.

Then he could work out the location of the roof windows. On the plans, he'd designed a skylight over the stairs and one in the bathroom, which was important because it could be opened to prevent mould. This removed the need to waste power on an electrical extraction fan, keeping the electrical wattage of daily running down as far as possible.

Near Miss

Near the end of this initial stage, on a day when Adam had a meeting booked with his electrician, he woke up feeling rough. Just a cold, he thought: there's no time for that. After the meeting, he felt worse; it felt more like 'flu heading his way, but he hoped an early night would see it off. The next morning he was worse still, necessitating a day in bed to recover, but by the night he could tell it was something serious.

Enfys made him call 111, as the top of his left leg was bright red and burning hot, and sensitive to the touch. He suspected shingles but 111 thought not. They were foxed, but said to go to A&E if it wasn't better in the morning.

The next day Adam was sweating, delirious and panicking, and he couldn't walk. He had to give in and go to A&E in Eastbourne, where they ran a load of tests and diagnosed cellulitis, which he'd never heard of. It's caused by a bacterial infection of the deeper layers of your skin cells. It's more likely to happen if the skin is broken, cracked or dry, and can become very serious, even fatal, if it spreads to the blood, muscles and bones. It was the strangest feeling, as though his body was shutting down. He was put on an antibiotic drip, which slowly stabilised his condition.

He was back at work on the build after a week, but it was a warning shot: he had to take better care of himself. Battling Ménière's on a daily basis, doing heavy physical work, living in a van through the winter – it was all only sustainable for so long. It's tempting to treat yourself like an infinite resource,

Illness stops play – Salbo licking Adam

but it doesn't work forever. Adam was far too busy to be able to afford to let illness get in the way, but it was time to start being more careful.

It was a relief to be able to start running again as his health improved: it's important for his state of mind. It wasn't quite the same as in the old days, when Salbo would run further and faster than him, shooting off to chase squirrels, jumping over any stiles they encountered. For the last eight months or so, she's struggled to keep up and can't jump so high. When Adam took her for a check-up, the vet said that, since she was about 15, she was too old to manage really long walks.

What's more, she lost her hearing quite suddenly a few months ago. That was a blow to Adam, especially because she'd been doing the listening for

115

both of them for a while, as his unofficial hearing dog. Enfys' ears will have to protect them all from knife-wielding nutters now, so she may need to forgo the fancy earplugs she wears to block out Adam's snoring!

Salbo's eyes aren't what they were either, so Adam will get to return the favour and look out for both of them. Thank goodness Devon kept insisting on a dog, because Salbo's really helped Adam through. He's feels lucky to have had her companionship this long and she still makes every day better.

- 8 -
Reclamation and Retro
Designing the cabin

CI and Scaffold Boards

Adam started the upstairs of the cabin by building all the walls, insulating heavily and adding a vapour barrier. This had three purposes: firstly, to stop it from being freezing in the winter, with as little wasteful heat-leakage as possible. Secondly, similar to the bus, the containers are made of metal, so they also need cooling in summer to stop them from becoming oppressively hot. Thirdly, it would help avoid condensation developing when warm air hits the colder metal surface. Otherwise, over time, moisture would trickle down the walls, pool at the bottom and create problematic rot and mould.

The plan was to also insulate the external walls between the metal and the wood cladding he would be attaching around the outside. One exception to this was the ground-floor wall with the front door in it. He wanted this left unclad to show the container's shipping number and its origin and character. To compensate for that he had to put double insulation on the inside, and use double-glazed aluminium windows. The floor and ceiling between the two storeys needed insulating too. He's delighted with how well it's worked. The insulation took a lot of time and money but Enfys took on most of the work to free Adam up for carpentry.

For the long internal walls, he decided to use plasterboard because it's pretty cheap and over the years he's come to enjoy plastering. Also, this time he wanted most of the interior to look more solid than a temporary structure like the double-decker. He was starting to feel his way into the aesthetic the cabin seemed to need, which was very different from the bus.

He used reclaimed scaffold boards for the internal woodwork because they're tough, cheap and have similar appeal to shipping containers: they both get moved around, and are used and reused to get things where they need to be, while keeping them safe. They both have a functional, simple design. The boards in the cabin had been used for years on scaffolds around London by a roofing company. You can see marks all over them where roof tiles have been cut with a grinder.

To make the wood go further, Adam had them split down the centre so that he got two lighter, thinner boards for the price of each heavy, thick one. He then sanded and oiled them and used them for doors, the ceiling of the bathroom and most of the other internal woodwork, including the built-in bed frames.

He's pleased with the results, especially where he used the boards to clad the stairwell to visually link the upper and lower containers. This emphasises the height of the structure from the floor, up the spiral, through the skylight to the trees beyond. It's quite inspiring – grand but also tactile and natural.

One particularly lucky purchase was a load of large sheets of corrugated iron, reclaimed from an old barn. Corrugated iron, CI to its fans, has quite the online community, with 66,000 members in the Corrugated Iron Appreciation Society, posting photographs of the stuff in various states of corrosion and weathering. Adam bought plenty: 35 sheets of the stuff, thinking he'd have far too much, but knowing he wouldn't be able to match it convincingly if it ran out part way through.

When the sheets showed up, they were covered in tar and rust, enough to cause quite a stir in the Facebook group, and Adam worried they were too far gone. No one would want to stay somewhere that felt dirty, but once installed as the ceiling throughout, they looked fabulous, with a sort of post-apocalyptic glamour. He'd miscalculated though, so far from having excess there wasn't enough. Luckily, he managed to do all the ceilings apart from the bathroom, where he used reclaimed scaffold boards instead.

The whole place was developing a coherent identity: historic charm and urban, industrial cool, complemented by curves and a feeling of comfort and efficiency. The corrugated iron and scaffold boards flaunt their origins and years of hard use, but Adam bought a brand-new boiler and radiators to make sure the cabin would be well heated and cosy. It was a relief not to have anything to do with log burners this time.

A large part of the cabin's appeal is to do with light. When working in the cabin, Adam noticed that the light rose at one end and set at the other, pouring sunrise through one bedroom's round window, then sunset through the other, so he called them the Sunrise Room and the Sunset Room. Having enjoyed the effects of the borrowed light from internal windows in the bus, he took this a step further in the cabin, commissioning Brighton artist Jessica Parkes to make bespoke stained-glass fanlights to go above the doors. The brief he gave her was a sunrise for the Sunrise Room, a sunset for the Sunset Room, and the Evergreen Cabin logo and woodland for the shower room.

She took it from there and they look fantastic, in vivid colours like 1930s ceramics – Clarice Cliff maybe – but also in a style similar to that he'd used for the bus and cabin logos. Each fanlight has a roundel to reference the round windows, within a rectangle to reference the cabin, and they splash warm lozenges of colour around the walls as the sunlight moves around the woodland.

For the shower room, inspired by the ceiling cladding, Adam used new, corrugated iron (galvanised, to protect it from rust) rather than tiles. This would ensure it was leak-free and easy to clean, while linking its aesthetic to the rest of the cabin. He bought a new shower tray and found a brilliant,

Stained glass fanlights over the doors to the Sunrise Room (top) and the shower room (bottom)

angular, 1970s powder-blue sink and toilet to make the room more interesting and playful. Papering the room with curvy, multicoloured 1970s wallpaper made the aesthetic a fusion of retro kitsch and industrial edge that came together really well. As the cabin started to look better and better, it became more fun to work on.

The bathroom

The second-hand kitchen, upcycled with copper-pipe handles

After pipework, electrics and insulation, it was time to put down a floor surface. He used engineering board, a chipboard used for flat roofs, bought second hand from someone who'd used it briefly as a temporary roof during a loft conversion. He coated it with hard-wearing floor varnish, so it would keep its looks.

This use of humble materials in a way that elevates them into a design feature is nothing new – architects have been doing it in posh kitchens for ages, and it's really an extension of a lot of modernist ideas, but it still feels clever when you're on a tight budget and it just looks and feels ace. The varied colours and textures in the space work well together, so that it feels welcoming even though it's mostly quite basic.

The kitchen units came from his friend Rod, who was installing new cabinets at home. They were going in a skip otherwise. Rod brought them down from Birmingham and Adam used what he could, fitting the black and wood-veneer units. There were some leftover scaffold boards, so he used some for the worktop and most of the rest for a breakfast bar, supported on scaffold poles.

Rather than chucking it, he even used the rectangular cutout of wood left over from fitting the sink to make bedside tables upstairs. For the kitchen splashback, he used up offcuts of the new corrugated iron bought for the shower, creating a cohesive, low-budget aesthetic throughout both floors. He finished off the space with a retro Smeg fridge he already had.

Coming Full Circle

Finishing touches included industrial-style light fittings, switches and sockets with surface rust on the casings. Enfys made all the door handles and the tap out of copper pipes, having learnt how to do it when they were converting the Luton van. The cabin's a far more grown-up looking space than the bus, its colourway mostly brown woods and black metal, but there's tons of light and many brighter accents, so it feels calm rather than dour.

There are a few links to the past in the cabin, here and there. With his great-grandfather's lovely old chair and a side table, Adam made a quiet reading nook under the curve of the stairs, where the wall is striped with shadows from the treads. The sofa bed he'd had in his flat before renting it out had been in storage all this time, waiting to go to France; this was a trip it would never take, but at least it could be put to use again in the cabin's lounge. He fitted blinds on the windows and built shelving into the end wall, and a shallow desk with a view through the round window. In pride of place on these shelves is Rob's socket, the one Mick sent to replace the one his family had hidden on the bus in memory of their son, years before.

There are also a few little souvenirs from the bus dotted around the place, since it's part of the cabin's past, but actually, by the time he was finishing the cabin, Adam found he'd moved on and didn't miss the bus any more. He was enjoying this bigger, less nostalgic, more stylish space. The bus was a good adventure, but it's best to look forwards.

The outside space is very important, especially since it's often quite outdoorsy people who visit the cabin. Adam managed to source some UK-grown larch boards to clad the outer walls of the containers. Larch is deciduous, but it's in the same Pinaceae family as the trees in the woodland; it's tough, waterproof, fairly resistant to rot and highly valued for external cladding and yachts. Larch was thought to protect against evil spirits in European folklore, but Adam will be satisfied if it protects against water. He wanted UK wood despite it having more knots than imported timber, because it has fewer air miles and is a bit cheaper, and has a high oil content. You don't need to treat it at all as a result. It protects itself from water for a decade if properly mounted with a membrane behind it.

Devon had played an important role in making the bus a success, helping decorate it, lending a hand with the changeovers, taking part in the TV appearances and so on. Adam likes to think that growing up with the bus project and being in the wood influenced her in her choice to study environmental science at Birmingham University. She applied her first-class degree as a research technician studying which plants would thrive in the various soil types along railway embankments, to help offset transport's carbon footprint. He was glad to find a way to tap into her expertise when building the cabin.

Salbo keeping watch at the cabin

Plum Pictures were keen to include her in the filming, since she was part of the earlier narrative too, a decade earlier, and it gave the story a pleasing symmetry and circularity, the child returning as an adult to finish the build. She was reluctant, partly because having worn her favourite T-shirt for the first programme, which said 'Sweet' on the front, she realised later that her cardigan had obscured the 's' and 't', leaving her wearing a 'wee' T-shirt potentially in front of millions of people forever. Adam pointed out that they hadn't even ended up using that footage, but she still wasn't keen, so Plum paid her travel

Devon and Adam atop the cabin, having laid the green roof

A drone shot showing how the green-roofed cabin blends into the woodland and how the brise-soleil looks from above

expenses and filmed at the weekend to persuade her. That means Devon got paid more than Adam did, which amuses her no end.

Because of her expertise with plants, Devon helped Adam to choose the green roof for the cabin. Adam wanted a living roof to help the cabin blend into its woodland surroundings. The plants were supplied by a great company called Green Roofs Direct in Ireland, which sells sedums laid out on rolls like turf. The roof adds insulation to the cabin too. Devon helped Adam to lay it, fitting it around the skylights and weighing it down with heavy pebbles along the edges.

Adam built a sun canopy projecting a couple of feet horizontally from the top of the cabin, all along the front. It was a planning condition that the cabin had to have louvres to create a brise-soleil, because there are bats in the woods and this will stop light pollution from ruining their habitat. It looks great, emphasising the width of the cabin and adding visual interest with ever-changing stripes of light and shadow, a visual rhyme with the striped shadows cast within the cabin every morning and evening by the staircase and the narrow tree trunks in the woodland.

There are plenty of outdoor details to make a stay at the cabin special: the wood-fired hot tub, a large decking area, benches and a picnic table, hammocks, potted bamboos, deckchairs, a glitterball and a big firepit with a tripod to hang a cooking pot from. In the private woodland that surrounds the cabin there's a den-building area and secret trails where you can really be at one with nature, watching deer, rabbits, squirrels and plenty of birdlife, and spotting fungi.

The hot tub and cabin at night

View of the cabin from the fire pit

Seating area at the front of the cabin

Cabin Fever

Interestingly, the cabin seems to attract a very different demographic from the bus. The bus really appealed to families and small groups, whereas the cabin is especially popular with couples. Adam's initial determination to make sure that his planning and size of structure allowed for a property that could sleep six seems to have been unnecessary after all. Since it's more sophisticated than the bus, the income works out similar, even with fewer guests. The locals must be delighted that the site has become even quieter, with fewer cars than before, and less disturbance of nature.

Londoners often come to the cabin, and a couple recently left him a note in the guestbook to say,

> *'The lack of light pollution helped us spot the International Space Station from the hot tub!'*

All the early reviews for the cabin have been just as good as for the bus, in fact:

> *'Beautiful place in a stunning location. Got lost for a good 3 hours in the local woods, wandered back and chilled out all day outside the cabin. It's been years since he's felt so peaceful. We'll be back for sure. What a magical place.'*

> *'Adam's cabin is fantastic and he is such a great host! The cabin is so cozy, there is everything you could need, and a lot of good restaurants and things nearby. It's a great place to light a bonfire, relax with a book, or enjoy the hot tub!'*

> *'We had such a lovely two night break. It felt much longer and that was because the cabin is such a comfortable and relaxing space. We didn't need to use our car once we were there... we walked in the woods, strolled to the pub and basked in the hot tub!'*

> *'If you are looking to switch off and reconnect with nature, then Evergreen Cabin is the place for you! The cabin is beautifully built in a private woodland and the simplicity of the interior space makes you feel totally at ease. We loved how many different outdoor spots there were to experience from the giant wood-fired hot tub under the trees, to lazing in the hammock with a book to cooking over the campfire. Even with heavy rain on one of the days during our stay, it was magical to sit inside drinking cups of tea whilst looking out through the trees through the many large windows that bring the outside in. We were even lucky enough to spot some deer in the neighbouring field – couldn't recommend this place enough for a full digital detox and reset!'*

Finishing in time for the TV reveal was a mad rush. Adam had a long snagging list to take care of – details here and there that needed to be just right. He couldn't have done it without Enfys, Devon and his sister Nadia's family: Nick, Rachel and Alice. He made time for the important things though, like having a new Hawaiian shirt printed for the occasion, with Salbo's silly face all over it.

This time, Jane Berry came to dress and style the place to a professional standard. Luckily, on reveal day, George was impressed – he's a genuine enthusiast and Adam was surprised by what an emotional experience it turned out to be, having been through the mill over the previous couple of years. When he posted a few shots on the cabin account, he was overwhelmed by the gush of congratulations and appreciation from the public. It's been a great place for him to be, on the rare occasions it doesn't have guests. Adam, Enfys and family very much enjoyed their Christmas 2023 there.

George and Adam chatting on reveal day

The family responsible for the bus fire continued to deny liability until February 2023, ten months after the blaze. It would have been so different, so much less upsetting, had they admitted liability in the face of such clear evidence. He wouldn't have had the worry of months of waiting and feeling suspected before they finally admitted what had happened.

Adam soon tired of fighting but the costs of the process and the income lost meant he couldn't afford to give up. Shortly before this book's publication, he heard that the case would likely have to go to court, as his attempts to settle had been rejected, so funding for that would have to be found. Downhearted but not beaten, he started to work on fundraising ideas. Sometimes it feels as though large corporations drag things out deliberately in the hope that claimants run out of money, but he was determined not to be priced out of justice.

Come March 2024, Adam was running out of money. He'd taken out short-term loans when the influencer guests had first admitted liability for the fire, thinking it would be over quickly. How wrong he was: the insurer's in-house forensic accountants and loss adjusters wore Adam down month after month, wasting time in the knowledge that every email and call his solicitor had to make was costing him money. With massive, ever-accumulating legal bills, he was also struggling to service the payments on the loans.

Adam's at least as stubborn as the next man and can dig in for a fight when he needs to, but it felt as though matters were coming to a head. He had to ask his mother to lend him money – again – as he was now £35,000 in debt and interest was accumulating faster than he could pay it. She insisted she understood and didn't mind but it felt to Adam like the last straw, as though everything was spiralling out of control.

It was time for him to do what he does best: think outside the box. This time, his inspiration didn't come from a book about sailing round the world, but a film about a revenge-fuelled vendetta. Having watched director Martin Campbell's 2017 action thriller *The Foreigner*, in which Guan (Jackie Chan) takes matters into his own hands, Adam was inspired to take guerilla action. He didn't resort to the explosive vigilantism of the film but, like Guan, he realised that he wasn't going to get anywhere through the official channels.

In that spirit, he asked himself a question: 'What do very rich influencers value the most?' He decided it was keeping their followers, so they'd be keen to avoid having their name dragged through the mud online, and every word of it true. Their following is their only source of income. He'd already suggested his solicitor write to the family to let them know about the insurance company's delays, but the solicitor resisted. Although he'd worked very hard to get a decent outcome for Adam, he was bound by especially cautious rules of engagement and has his reputation to protect.

Adam asked his solicitor to do one last job: find out how long he had to take the claim to court before it timed out due to limitation. The answer was that he had six years from the date of the fire, two years earlier. The solicitor suggested starting no later than a year before the deadline. That gave Adam two to three years to raise the money for a court case, estimated at £70,000. That wouldn't be possible without a massive crowdfunder. There was good reason to go to trial, as even more of his losses would by then have become clear, evidenced and claimable. The only way he could make a crowdfunder work was by getting the attention of enough people, such as straight after the screening of series 12 of *George Clarke's Amazing Spaces.*

However, he and I were both keen to direct any public interest the TV programme generated in the cabin towards this book, hoping some fans of the show might be interested in Adam's story. Of course, he also hoped it would stimulate holiday bookings at the cabin. Encouraging anyone who searched for the Evergreen Cabin website to engage in a crowdfunder instead would at least dilute those chances. Also, legal cases absorb not only funds but attention and positive state of mind, focusing as they do on negative events in the past. Adam decided to do everything he could to settle out of court.

Since official channels had failed, it was time to go off-road. To start with, Adam settled up his legal bill and disinstructed the solicitor. Next, he sent a very frank email to the insurance company's loss adjuster, mentioning the book, the TV programme and the crowdfunder. Desperate in the face of ruin, he explained that, although the book and TV show don't name the influencers, he'd have no choice but to give more detail in the crowdfunder campaign, should a suitable settlement not be urgently forthcoming, as his back was against the wall. Channelling Chan, he sent a copy of the email to the family directly, having not contacted them since the time of the fire. He thought they might not even realise he was still waiting, and hoped they'd instruct their solicitor to pressure the insurance company to settle. The final step was inspired by the fact that Adam's neighbours' initial hostility to himself and the bus did eventually soften in the face of his relentless good cheer a decade earlier. He began a daily campaign of friendly, polite but very insistent communication with the loss adjuster.

It took about a week and a half before anything happened, and then the offer came in. Adam counter-offered and a deal was struck, allowing him to rid himself of all his debts, avoid the need for a court case and allow him to put the matter behind him once and for all. History does not relate what catalysed this change: whether the influencers got involved, or Fortuna, or the poor, maddened loss adjuster, who was used to solicitors and couldn't understand the rules by which Adam was playing. There was no way to tell how far he'd go or whether he'd ever give up. I'm not sure he knew himself.

Either way, Adam was proved right: a creative, direct, risky, instinctive approach was the only way out of the deadlock. It seems fitting that the bus adventure should close, much as it started, and like the builds and most other things in his life, with Adam playing it by ear.

Epilogue

Next Stop

Though his dad Brian didn't play any instruments, he was always advising Adam to 'Just play it by ear, son,' hence the title of this book. He lived his own life like that, with unpredictable results. I'll give you one example, enough to show that the apple hasn't fallen far from the tree. When he decided that their family home was a bit cramped for the four of them (himself, mum Evelyn, big sister Nadia and Adam), Brian took action.

He decided they needed an extension to their house. As a desk-bound pen-pusher for a pharmaceuticals company, he had no training or experience in architecture, drafting, planning or building, but he didn't let that get in the way of him doing it all himself. Remind you of anyone? Now you know where Adam gets it from. To be fair, this extension to the garage became a dining room that is still there today, but it didn't always look as though it would turn out that way: there were some hairy moments.

Half the neighbourhood turned out to watch the spectacle of Brian using the family's army-green Hillman Minx to push down the wall at the back of his garage at the start of the project, only to be horrified when it fell backwards rather than forwards. The front of the car, and his dad within it, were buried in rubble. Friends dug them out to find there wasn't a scratch on either of them. He'd always said that car was like a tank.

Brian driving the kids in 'The Tank' Hillman Minx

Brian, with the help of Evelyn and his friend Pete, dug the footings by hand to save money. They were doing alright, digging the metre-deep trench until they discovered an unexploded WWII bomb down there. Bomb disposal arrived in all their gear and glory, to discover that they'd been called to defuse an old can of paint.

When it was concrete time, Brian overestimated the amount needed. He poured out the surplus onto a tarpaulin on the driveway but, since the drive sloped down to the house, the quick-drying concrete slid down to the garage door and sealed it shut for weeks. The car was stuck in there, so the kids had to walk to school until Brian had hired a Kango drill to release it.

None of this stopped him. He never gave up on his bonkers schemes: Adam loves him for that and many other things. Brian must have enjoyed getting hands-on with that extension, because later on he left his desk job and took up painting and decorating. Two years after he helped Adam decorate the bus for its big reveal, he was diagnosed with cancer in his lung and pancreas, and died two years later, in 2017. Adam's glad Brian got to see the bus become successful, and thankful that he taught him to play it by ear.

Like Brian, Adam likes to always have a project on the go, but he isn't sure what will come next. He needs to focus on his existing business first. Right now, the cabin has had a clean run of five-star reviews for its first few months of rentals. He's delighted that people enjoy it, but there's a lot of competition in the holiday rentals marketplace, and it's hard to sustain momentum without lots of cash to spend on marketing. Bookings are not yet filled as far ahead as he'd like, but it has potential and, with luck, the screening of series 12 of *George Clarke's Amazing Spaces* will happen at some point, and that may help.

Devon has just headed off round the world on a low-budget adventure of her own, to stay with host families everywhere from the Philippines to Fiji. Adam suggested fondly that she was taking after her old man, but she's having none of it, listing differences including detailed planning, proper job, qualifications...

So, where does this all leave us? Have Adam and I reassured you that the kind of perilous escapade he considers an adventure is something you'd rather do without, thank you very much? You don't think your life would be enriched by battles with neighbours, machinery and planning committees, or by near-constant uncertainty?

Or have we given you a taste for it, convinced you to dive in headfirst when you next have a mad idea, because existence tastes more like life, more vital and undiluted that way? Would you be happier catching a wave and crashing than watching someone else do it from the safety of your sofa? If so, then we wish you all the best in pursuing whatever crackpot scheme you dream up. It won't be easy, but you might have fun playing it by ear, and if you keep going, you may get through it alive with a tale to tell. Good luck. Forward, to adventure!

PS from Adam

This book project has been surprisingly liberating. Mima approached me a few years ago, to ask whether I'd be interested in putting together a book of my exploits. I thought that would be cool, then forgot about it. I remember the morning clearly when, running along the beautiful Croatian coastline, it felt right all of a sudden.

I didn't want to write it myself and wouldn't have the time once I started building the cabin, so I started recording hours of thoughts for Mima. She was the perfect person to ask the right questions, bring order to my chaotic ramblings, and pull out the story within them. She's an old friend, a writer and the most intelligent person I know. Also, she knows some of the stories better than I do, reminding me of some I'd forgotten, on the verge of being lost to me forever.

My dad once spent months writing a memoir by hand on A4 lined paper when I was about 12. He used to read me parts of it, and I loved hearing about his adventures in and around bombed out buildings in South London. Imagine my shock when I came into the living room one morning to find him burning page after page in the fireplace. The whole thing went up in smoke, so I cried and he was angry. Now I realise his life wasn't all fun and laughs. Maybe he'd reached a painful part of his life story that upset him enough to destroy it all, but I still feel sad that I never got to read it. He's dead now and I've all but forgotten those stories he told me. Maybe the darker parts would have explained why he sometimes flew into rages and occasionally found it hard not to bear grudges.

Perhaps writing and burning the memories was therapy enough for him, but I was determined not to do that myself. Sometimes, I was tempted to focus on darker moments, but then I'd remember positive things too. As the story gradually appeared on paper in front of me, I started to feel good about it, and hoped it might inspire other people too. The dishonesty of the people who caused the loss of the bus is the exception, not the rule. Loss adjusters may work for massive corporations with questionable ethics, but it's just a job, they're just people, with families and everyday problems like everyone else.

I wanted the book to be positive, accepting, forgiving, something to make me and readers stronger. We have the power to move forwards even in awful circumstances. Start small. You'll find a way. It's in all of us. Because we're a long time dead, our time is now, so grab it with both hands.

Adam

Mima Biddulph

After reading English literature at Newnham College, Cambridge, Mima wrote poetry, features and travel pieces for print media. She trained as a barrister then as a teacher, and for 20 years taught literature and history of art. She is structural editor of several non-fiction titles, including Oliver James' *Sunday Times* bestseller *Affluenza*, which she also abridged for audiobook recording.

Mima and Adam have been friends since the nineties, so she knows his story and its context inside out, and was involved in the rebirth of the bus after the first fire. They worked together for over a year to capture this story.

Mima recently completed Curtis Brown Creative's flagship, six-month Writing Your Novel course. She has written two novels, a collection of short stories, several plays, musicals and songs. She lives in Kingston. Visit mimabiddulph.com to learn more or follow her on Facebook (mima.biddulph) or Instagram (@mima.biddulph).

Bookings: evergreencabin.co.uk

 greenbusman

 @evergreen_cabin

BV - #0035 - 130624 - C0 - 234/156/10 - PB - 9781068614903 - Matt Lamination